Crazy Dumplings II:

Amanda Roberts

Two Americans in China Press
Oviedo, FL

http://www.twoamericansinchina.com/
© 2016 Amanda Roberts

Photos © 2015 Ruth Silbermeyr-Song
http://www.chinaelevatorstories.com/

Cover design & other images © 2015 Cherith Vaughan
http://cherithana.wix.com/portfolio

All rights reserved. No part of this publication may be reproduced or transmitted in any form or by any means, electronic or mechanical, including photocopying, recording, or any information storage or retrieval system, without express written permission from the publisher.

ISBN: 978-0-9907753-4-8

Table of Contents

Introduction 1
Cooking Notes 2
Folding Dumplings 6
Basic Dumpling Wrapper 9
Savory Dumplings 10
Simple Chinese Dumplings 11
Artichoke Dumplings 13
Avocado Chipotle Chicken Dumplings 14
Bacon Cheeseburger Dumplings 16
Balsamic Bleu Cheese Rib-eye Steak Dumplings 18
Bang Bang Shrimp Dumplings 20
Basil Cashew Chicken Dumplings 22
Basil Pesto and Feta Dumplings 24
Beef and Veggie Dumplings 27
Bierock Dumplings 29
Cha Gio Viet Dumplings 31
Cheese and Mushroom Dumplings 33
Cheesy Breakfast Dumplings 35
Cheesy Potato Crawfish Dumplings 37
Chicken, Corn, and Cilantro Dumplings 39
Chicken Enchilada Dumplings 41
Chinese Veggie Dumplings 43
Chorizo Breakfast Dumplings 45
Citrus-Herb Salmon Dumplings 47

Coconut Lime Chicken Dumplings 49

Cola Chinese Chicken Dumplings 51

Creamed Spinach with Pork Dumplings 53

Creamy Tuna Dumplings 55

Delicious Turkey Dumplings 56

Easy Chinese Chicken Dumplings 58

Eggplant Ricotta Dumplings 62

Eggs Benedict Dumplings 64

Firecracker Chicken Dumplings 66

Fresh Spring Chicken Dumplings 68

Fried Pickle Dumplings 70

Guacamole Dumplings 71

General Tsao's Dumplings 73

Grilled Cheese Tomato Soup Dumplings 75

Ham and Honey Mustard Dumplings 76

Honey Pepper Salmon Dumplings 78

Hummus, Crab, and Jalapeno Dumplings 81

Jalapeño Chicken Dumplings 83

Kimchee Bokkeumbap Dumplings 85

Korean Fried Chicken (KFC) Dumplings 87

Lamb with Pomegranate Salsa Dumplings 89

Lobster Cream Cheese Dumplings 91

Nepali Momos 95

Pecan Chicken Dumplings 97

Philly Cheese Steak Pho Dumplings 98

Porcupine Meatball Dumplings 100

Pork with Mango Salsa Dumplings 102

Crazy Dumplings

Pumpkin and Potato Dumplings 104

Red Cooked Chicken Dumplings 106

Reindeer Mushroom Dumplings 108

Savory Crab Dumplings 112

Sesame Chicken Dumplings 114

Seitan Fajita Dumplings 116

Spiced Pork Dumplings 118

Spicy Peanut Shrimp Dumplings 120

Spicy Ramen Egg Dumplings 123

Spicy Shrimp with Avocado Lime Sauce Dumplings 125

Sriracha Lime Chicken Dumplings 127

Sweet and Tangy Tuna Dumplings 129

Tandoori Chicken Dumplings 131

Thai Chicken Dumplings 133

Tofu, Veggie, and Peanut Dumplings 135

Turkey Bacon Stuffed Dumplings 137

Uzbek Manti 138

Vietnamese Meatball Mango Dumplings 140

Sweet Dumplings 142

Banana Cream Dumplings 143

Blackberry Dumplings 144

Blueberry Cream Dumplings 146

Chocolate Covered Cherry Dumplings 148

Kaya Dumplings 150

Peach Pie Dumplings 154

Peanut Butter Chocolate Dumplings 155

Prune Dumplings with Toffee Sauce 156

Pumpkin Cream Cheese Dumplings	158
Strawberry Cheesecake Dumplings	161
Sweet Rice and Raisin Dumplings	162
Sweet Tomato Dumplings	164
Tropical Fruit Dumplings	166
Sauces	167
Alfredo Dipping Sauce	168
Avocado Lime Sauce	169
Chinese Chili Sauce	170
Chipotle Mayonnaise	172
Green Cashew Sauce	173
Lingonberry Sauce	174
Honey Chipotle Sauce	175
Nuoc Cham (Vietnamese Spicy Fish Sauce)	176
Porcupine Dipping Sauce	177
Salsa	178
Thai Sweet Chili Sauce	180
Wasabi Mayo	181
Metric Conversions	182
Volume Conversions	183
Weight Conversions	184
Oven Temperature Conversions	185
About the Author	186
Thank You!	187

Introduction

I knew before I even finished writing my first Crazy Dumplings cookbook that I would have to write another one. There were simply far too many amazing possibilities out there for dumplings to contain them all in one book.

I also wanted to research more about dumplings and pocket foods around the world. While the first book had a couple of internationally inspired recipes, this one goes much further. In the time since the first dumpling book was published, I've been able to travel quite a bit, and you can feel those other cultures in this book. There are several dumplings inspired by Vietnam and Thailand, but through research I have found dumplings all over the world – from Nepal to Uzbekistan to Germany. And those inspirations found a home in *Crazy Dumplings II* as well.

I hope you enjoy your culinary journey through *Crazy Dumplings II: Even Dumplinger*. I can't wait to see where dumplings will take us next!

Cooking Notes

Servings

All of the following recipes are for 12 dumplings, which is just about perfect for a dinner for two. You can easily double or triple the ingredients to make large quantities of dumplings for families or get-togethers. You can also make smaller dumplings (only ½ inch in diameter dough balls) as hors d'oeuvres for parties.

Dumpling Wrappers

In America and China, dumplings have become so popular that the wrappers can easily be bought already prepared. While these can significantly cut down your cooking time, I prefer making my own because they are thicker and taste better. Even in China, every time we go to restaurants that are "famous" for their dumplings, what usually sets their dumplings apart is homemade dumpling wrappers.

Cooking Time

The cooking time for all of these recipes is about 45-60 minutes depending on how you cook your dumplings. While mixing the flour and water to make the dumplings doesn't take long, you have to wait 15 minutes for the dough to set up. Rolling out the dough takes another 15 minutes. Frying the dumplings takes about 5 minutes, but boiling or steaming them takes about another 10 minutes. Of course, if you use commercial dumpling wrappers, this time is significantly reduced.

The Wok

It is easiest to fry a dumpling in a wok. The round shape and even cooking temperature of a wok is perfect for creating golden brown dumplings. Carbon steel woks are the best as they heat and cool quickly. If you use a gas range, you can use a round or flat bottom wok; if you use an electric range, you will want a flat bottom wok. Both conduct heat evenly, but a round bottom wok will redirect too much heat back to the range on an electric stove and can damage the heating elements.

Cooking

Almost all of the recipes in the book are for fried dumplings. Fried dumplings tend to taste the best, look the best, and have the best texture. However, many can also be steamed or boiled. Here are the three ways you can cook your dumplings:

1. To fry dumplings, preheat 1 cup of oil for 30 seconds on high heat, then lower heat to medium. Cook dumplings on each side for about 3 minutes or until golden brown.
2. To steam dumplings, place in a steamer basket or on an elevated plate in a wok over water on high heat for about 10 minutes.
3. To boil dumplings, place in boiling water for about 10 minutes.
4. Always cut a dumpling open and check to make sure it is cooked through, especially when using a meat filling.

Freezing and Leftovers

Once you prepare the dumplings, but before you cook them, they can be frozen and kept for several weeks. Place the prepared dumplings on a cookie sheet and put them into the freezer for 15 minutes. Then, put the frozen dumplings into a freezer bag and place them back into the freezer. When cooking the frozen dumplings, do not thaw, but cook immediately. Preparing large batches of dumplings is a great weekend activity for families so they can then have pre-made, but homemade, snacks ready to go for the kids all week or as emergency dinner ideas.

Cooked leftover dumplings can be refrigerated for a day or two and reheated in an oven at 350 degrees for 10 minutes.

Filling Ingredients

To help make my instructions more succinct, many times I will say something like "add all filling ingredients." Typically, this will mean everything listed except the dumpling wrappers, frying oil, and dipping sauces, unless otherwise noted.

Also, many of the ingredients need to be chopped, minced, diced, or finely sliced small enough that the ingredients can be mixed together. I simplified the directions for these ingredients as "chopped," but however you slice or dice it, make sure that you are able to get a little of everything in each dumpling.

Meat

While this book contains quite a few vegetarian recipes, many recipes contain meat. But that doesn't mean that vegetarians can't enjoy them! All of the recipes here are flexible and open to your own interpretation, so feel free to make them your own. All of the recipes that call for ground meat can use tofu crumbles instead. You can also use seitan as a substitute for chicken. If any of these

Crazy Dumplings

recipes contain an ingredient you don't like or can't find where you live, you can almost always cut it out or find a suitable alternative. Flexibility is the most important ingredient in the kitchen.

Folding Dumplings

I will be the first to admit that I am terrible at folding dumplings. I'm not an artist, so making lovely folds and artistic designs just isn't in me. For me, a "dumplinger" (a little plastic tool for folding and crimping dumplings and the inspiration for this book's subtitle) is the best way for me to fold dumplings. However, there are a few easy folds that even I can do and have illustrated for you below.

The Simple Fold

Crazy Dumplings

The Pyramid

The Loop

You can find lots more examples of folded dumplings on my Pinterest page (http://www.pinterest.com/amandachina/crazy-dumplings/). Feel free to experiment with your own dumpling folding styles and be sure to send me pictures!

Basic Dumpling Wrapper

This recipe is for making 12 dumpling wrappers, enough for all the dumpling filling recipes in this book. Keep some extra flour on hand for flouring the counter and your hands to keep everything from sticking. Also, feel free to add more flour if necessary if the dough is too sticky.

- 3/4 cup flour
- 1/3 cup boiling water
- Dash of salt
- Flour for dusting

1. In a bowl, mix flour and salt together.
2. Slowly drizzle in water, mixing with a chopstick or fork.
3. Leave the mixture in the bowl, covered with plastic wrap, for 15 minutes.
4. Gather the dough up into a ball and knead for a minute or two until the dough is smooth.
5. Pinch off a small portion of dough and roll into a ball about 1 inch in diameter. Roll out into a flat circle with a rolling pin, dusting the pin and surface with flour to keep dough from sticking.
6. Choose a dumpling filling from elsewhere in this book and continue following the directions there.

Amanda Roberts

Savory Dumplings

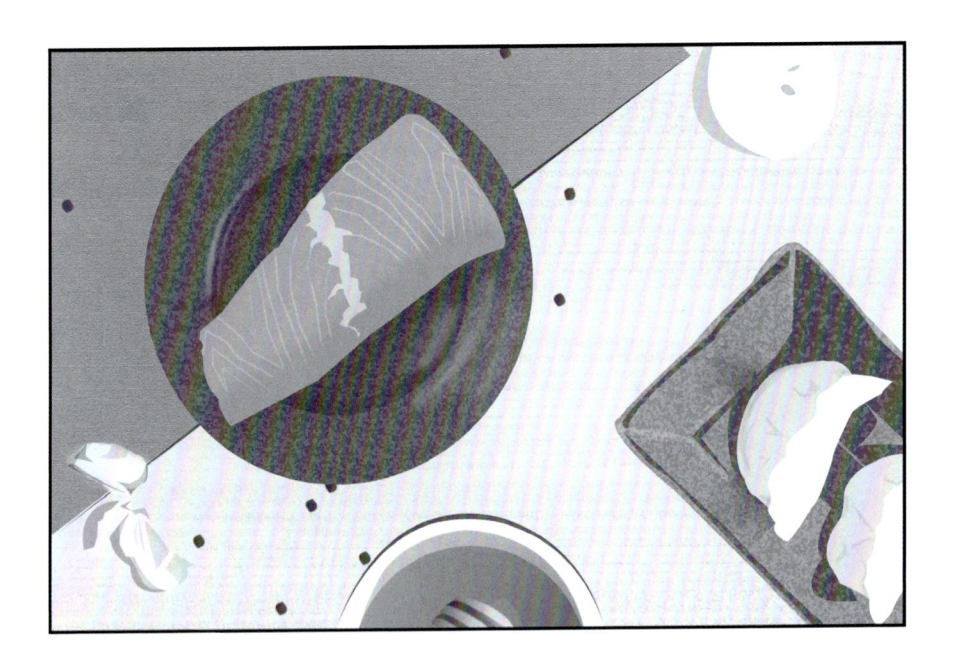

Crazy Dumplings

Simple Chinese Dumplings

Fresh ginger has a very strong taste. The last thing you want to do is bite into a chunk of fresh ginger! I always use a microplane to shred the ginger as small as possible. I use a garlic press to get the most flavor out of fresh garlic.

- 1 cup ground meat
- 1 tsp ginger, microplaned
- 1 garlic clove, pressed
- 1 green onion, chopped
- 12 dumpling wrappers
- 1 cup of oil, if frying
- Soy Sauce, Thai Sweet Chili Sauce, or Chinese Chili Sauce (See recipes in the Sauces section)

1. Mix meat and spices together.
2. Spoon mixture into dumpling wrappers and pinch closed.
3. Cook dumplings.
   a. To fry dumplings, preheat oil in a wok for 30 seconds on high heat, then lower heat to medium. Cook dumplings on each side for about 3 minutes or until golden brown.
   b. To steam dumplings, place in a steamer basket or on an elevated plate in a wok over water on high heat for about 10 minutes.
   c. To boil dumplings, place in boiling water for about 10 minutes.

4. Always cut a dumpling open to make sure it is cooked through.
5. Serve hot with soy sauce, Thai Sweet Chili Sauce, or Chinese Chili Sauce for dipping.

Artichoke Dumplings

This vegetarian recipe will remind you of creamy artichoke dip. It is a great party recipe that is sure to please!

- ½ cup artichoke hearts
- ¼ cup mozzarella
- ¼ cup canned spinach
- 2 garlic cloves, pressed
- 2 Tbsp parmesan cheese
- 1 Tbsp Chipotle Mayonnaise (recipe in the Sauces section)
- 12 dumpling wrappers
- 1 cup of oil
- Extra Chipotle Mayonnaise for dipping

1. In a bowl, blend artichoke hearts, mozzarella, spinach, garlic, parmesan, and 1 Tbsp Chipotle Mayonnaise together.
2. Spoon mixture into dumpling wrappers and pinch closed.
3. To fry dumplings, preheat oil in a wok for 30 seconds on high heat, then lower heat to medium. Cook dumplings on each side for about 3 minutes or until golden brown.
4. Serve hot with extra Chipotle Mayonnaise for dipping.

Amanda Roberts

🥑 Avocado Chipotle Chicken Dumplings 🥑

I love avocados, so I was sure to include a lot of recipes with avocadoes this time around. This dumpling is creamy enough it doesn't need extra dipping sauce.

- 1 avocado, peeled and pitted
- ¼ cup cilantro, chopped
- 3 Tbsp chipotle powder or sauce
- Juice of 1 lime
- ½ tsp cumin
- ½ tsp salt
- 3 Tbsp water
- 1 garlic clove, pressed
- 1 cup cooked chicken, chopped
- 12 dumpling wrappers
- 1 cup of oil

1. In a bowl, mash avocado and then whisk with cilantro, chipotle, juice, cumin, salt, water, and garlic.
2. Blend sauce together with chicken.
3. Spoon mixture into dumpling wrappers and pinch closed.

Crazy Dumplings

4. To fry dumplings, preheat oil in a wok for 30 seconds on high heat, then lower heat to medium. Cook dumplings on each side for about 3 minutes or until golden brown.
5. Serve hot.

Amanda Roberts

🐄 Bacon Cheeseburger Dumplings 🐷

These little darlings are great party favors. Lay out a tray of condiments and let everyone dip their burgers just the way they like them! Use your favorite cheese or make a variety with different cheese to really impress.

- 1 cup ground beef
- ¼ cup cheese, shredded
- 2 Tbsp fried bacon, chopped
- 1 garlic clove, pressed
- Dash of salt
- Dash of pepper
- 2 Tbsp onion, chopped (optional)
- 2 Tbsp pickles, chopped (optional)
- 12 dumpling wrappers
- 1 cup of oil
- Optional dips: mayonnaise, Chipotle Mayonnaise, Wasabi Mayonnaise, mustard, ketchup, Porcupine Dipping Sauce (recipes in the Sauces section)

1. In a bowl, combine the ground beef, cheese, bacon, garlic, salt and pepper, and onion and pickle if desired. Blend well.
2. Spoon mixture into dumpling wrappers and pinch closed.

Crazy Dumplings

3. To fry dumplings, preheat oil in a wok for 30 seconds on high heat, then lower heat to medium. Cook dumplings on each side for about 3 minutes or until golden brown.
4. Always cut a dumpling open to make sure it is cooked through.
5. Serve hot with optional sauces for dipping.

Amanda Roberts

Balsamic Bleu Cheese Rib-eye Steak Dumplings

Kickstarter backer Anthony Ryan Ortiz requested a recipe made with rib-eye steak. I'm not a big steak eater, but this recipe came out amazing.

- 1 cup rib-eye meat, chopped
- 1 cup balsamic vinegar
- ¼ cup red wine
- 1 Tbsp ground black pepper
- Dash of salt
- 1 Tbsp oil
- ½ cup balsamic vinegar
- ¼ cup bleu cheese, crumbled
- 12 dumpling wrappers
- 1 cup of oil

1. In a bowl, combine meat, 1 cup of vinegar, wine, pepper and salt. Let meat marinade for about an hour.
2. Heat 1 Tbsp of oil in wok. Remove meat from marinade and sauté in oil until cooked to desired color. Remove meat from heat and cool enough for handling.
3. In a bowl, blend ½ cup of vinegar and cheese together. Add meat and blend.

Crazy Dumplings

4. Spoon mixture into dumpling wrappers and pinch closed.
5. To fry dumplings, preheat oil in a wok for 30 seconds on high heat, then lower heat to medium. Cook dumplings on each side for about 3 minutes or until golden brown.
6. Serve hot.

Amanda Roberts

Bang Bang Shrimp Dumplings

These easy dumplings are packed with flavor! They are spicy but also a little sweet. So yummy!

- 1 Tbsp oil
- 1 cup shrimp, peeled, deveined, chopped
- ¼ cup cabbage, chopped
- ¼ cup avocado, mashed
- 2 Tbsp mayonnaise
- 1 Tbsp Sriracha
- ½ Tbsp Thai Sweet Chili Sauce (premade or use recipe in the Sauces section)
- Dash of salt
- Dash of cayenne pepper
- 12 dumpling wrappers
- 1 cup of oil, if frying

1. In a wok, heat oil. Add shrimp, salt, and cayenne pepper. Sauté until shrimp is cooked though. Add cabbage and sauté until wilted, only a moment. Remove from heat.
2. In a bowl, mix avocado, mayonnaise, Sriracha, and Thai Sweet Chili Sauce. Add shrimp mixture.
3. Spoon mixture into dumpling wrappers and pinch closed.

Crazy Dumplings

4. To fry dumplings, preheat oil in a wok for 30 seconds on high heat, then lower heat to medium. Cook dumplings on each side for about 3 minutes or until golden brown.
5. Serve hot.

Amanda Roberts

Basil Cashew Chicken Dumplings

One of my favorite dishes at our local Malaysian restaurant is basil chicken. I get a whole plate of it just for me! This recipe is sure to be just as addicting.

- 1 Tbsp Nuoc Cham (spicy fish sauce, recipe in the Sauces section)
- 1 Tbsp soy sauce
- ½ Tbsp Thai Sweet Chili Sauce (recipe in the Sauces section)
- ½ Tbsp brown sugar
- 1 garlic clove, pressed
- Splash of water
- 1 Tbsp oil
- ½ cup chicken, chopped
- ¼ cup red onion, chopped
- ½ cup packed Thai basil leaves, chopped
- ¼ cup packed lemon basil leaves, chopped
- ¼ cup roasted unsalted cashews, crushed
- 12 dumpling wrappers
- 1 cup of oil

Crazy Dumplings

1. In a wok, whisk together Nuoc Cham, soy sauce, Thai Sweet Chili Sauce, brown sugar, water, garlic, and oil.
2. Heat sauce. Then add chicken and red onion. Sauté until chicken is cooked and onion is tender.
3. Add in basil leaves and sauté until wilted. Remove from heat and let cool. Drain off extra sauce and reserve. Toss chicken with cashews.
4. Spoon mixture into dumpling wrappers and pinch closed.
5. To fry dumplings, preheat oil in a wok for 30 seconds on high heat, then lower heat to medium. Cook dumplings on each side for about 3 minutes or until golden brown.
6. Serve hot with reserved sauce for dipping.

Amanda Roberts

Basil Pesto and Feta Dumplings

Kickstarter backer Candace Fetzer noticed that many dumplings are made with cold weather in mind. After all, dumplings were invented to help fight frostbite! So she requested a light yet filling. I think this dumpling is just perfect for warmer weather.

- ½ can of chickpeas, 7.5 oz, drained
- ¼ cup basil leaves
- 1 garlic clove
- 1 Tbsp olive oil
- 1 Tbsp tahini
- Juice of 1 lemon
- Dash of salt
- ¼ cup yellow corn
- ¼ cup black beans, cooked
- ¼ cup red onion, chopped
- ¼ cup cilantro, chopped
- ¼ cup feta cheese, crumbled
- 12 dumpling wrappers
- 1 cup of oil

Crazy Dumplings

1. In a blender, add chickpeas, basil leaves, garlic clove, olive oil, tahini, lemon juice, and salt. Blend until smooth.
2. In a bowl, mix hummus with remaining dumpling filling ingredients.
3. Spoon mixture into dumpling wrappers and pinch closed.
4. To fry dumplings, preheat oil in a wok for 30 seconds on high heat, then lower heat to medium. Cook dumplings on each side for about 3 minutes or until golden brown.
5. Serve hot.

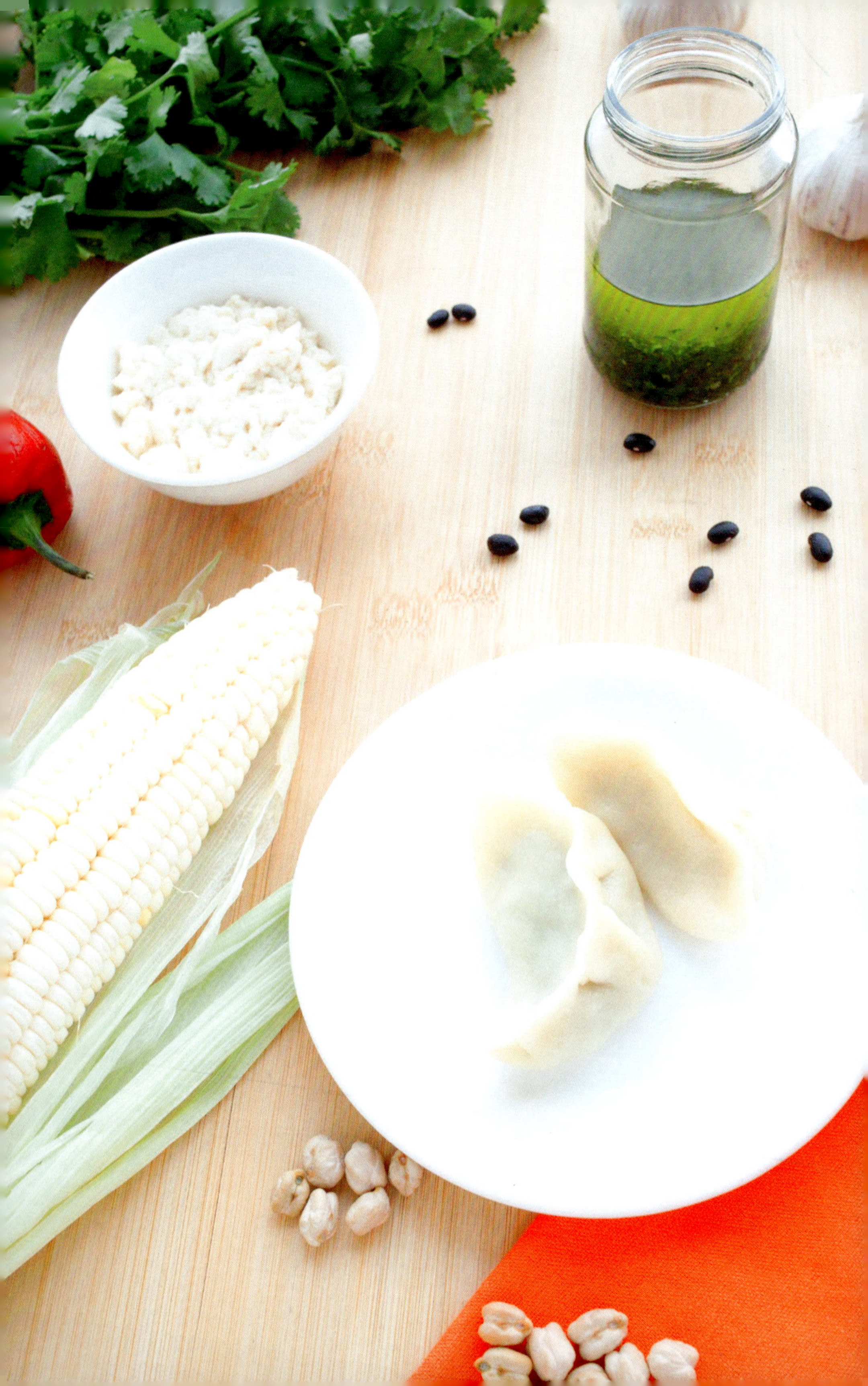

Beef and Veggie Dumplings

You can use any kind of beef in this recipe, but sliced steak or beef tips would be preferable. These heavy dumplings would be perfect for dinner. Serve with a side of steamed green veggies and mashed potatoes!

- 1 cup beef, chopped
- Dash of Salt
- Dash of Pepper
- 1 Tbsp oil
- ½ cup Burgundy or pinot noir
- 1 Tbsp beef bouillon
- 2 Tbsp tomato paste
- 2 bay leaves
- 1 tsp thyme
- ¼ cup carrots, chopped
- ¼ cup mushrooms, chopped
- 12 dumpling wrappers
- 1 cup of oil

Amanda Roberts

1. Lightly dust the meat with salt and pepper and set aside.
2. In a wok, whisk together oil, Burgundy/wine, bullion, tomato paste, leaves, and thyme.
3. Add meat and vegetables to wine sauce and sauté until veggies are tender and meat reaches desired brownness.
4. Drain sauce from meat mixture and reserve. Discard bay leaves.
5. After mixture cools, spoon mixture into dumpling wrappers and pinch closed.
6. To fry dumplings, preheat oil in a wok for 30 seconds on high heat, then lower heat to medium. Cook dumplings on each side for about 3 minutes or until golden brown.
7. Serve hot with excess wine sauce for dipping.

Crazy Dumplings

Bierock Dumplings

Bierocks are a type of German pocket food usually made with a meat-based filling inside a bread-like wrapper, more like a Chinese baozi than a jiaozi. This bierock-inspired dumpling is for Kickstarter backer Zach Brumleve.

- ½ cup ground meat
- ¼ cup onion, chopped
- ¼ cup cabbage, chopped
- 1 Tbsp Worcestershire sauce
- 1 tsp sugar
- Dash of Salt
- Dash of ground pepper
- ¼ cup mozzarella cheese, shredded
- 12 dumpling wrappers
- 1 cup of oil, if frying
- Chipotle Chili Sauce (recipe in the Sauces section)

1. In a wok, add meat, onion, cabbage, Worchester sauce, sugar, salt, and pepper. Brown meat.
2. **Remove from heat and add cheese. Blend well.**
3. Spoon mixture into dumpling wrappers and pinch closed.
4. Cook dumplings.
    a. To fry dumplings, preheat oil in a wok for 30 seconds on high heat, then lower heat to medium. Cook dumplings on

each side for about 3 minutes or until golden brown.

    b. To steam dumplings, place in a steamer basket or on an elevated plate in a wok over water on high heat for about 10 minutes.

5. Serve hot with Chipotle Chili Sauce for dipping.

Cha Gio Viet Dumplings

Cha Gong Viet is a Vietnamese spring roll that is served with Nuoc Cham, a spicy fish sauce. Feel free to use imitation krab instead of real crab if you need to. You can find the recipe for the sauce in the Sauces section.

- ¼ cup vermicelli noodles (sotanghon)
- ¼ cup ground lean pork
- ¼ cup shitake mushrooms, chopped
- ¼ cup white onion, chopped
- 2 garlic cloves, pressed
- ¼ cup crab meat, chopped
- ¼ cup shrimp, shelled and chopped
- ¼ teaspoon black pepper
- 1 Tbsp cilantro, chopped
- Juice of 1 lime
- 12 dumpling wrappers
- 1 cup of oil, if frying
- Nuoc Cham, spicy fish sauce, for dipping (recipe in the Sauces section)

1. Soak noodles in warm water for 20 minutes. Remove from water and finely chop.
2. Mix the noodles and the remaining filling ingredients

together.
3. Spoon mixture into dumpling wrappers and pinch closed.
4. Cook dumplings.
    a. To fry dumplings, preheat oil in a wok for 30 seconds on high heat, then lower heat to medium. Cook dumplings on each side for about 3 minutes or until golden brown.
    b. To steam dumplings, place in a steamer basket or on an elevated plate in a wok over water on high heat for about 10 minutes.
5. Always cut a dumpling open to make sure it is cooked through.
6. Serve hot with Nuoc Cham for dipping.

Cheese and Mushroom Dumplings

This vegetarian dumpling would make a great breakfast dumpling. Customize it by using your favorite kind of cheese.

- 1 Tbsp butter
- ½ cup fresh mushrooms, chopped
- ¼ cup green onions, chopped
- ¼ cup cheese, shredded
- 1 Tbsp basil
- ¼ cup heavy cream
- Dash of salt
- 12 dumpling wrappers
- 1 cup of oil, if frying

1. In a wok, melt the butter. Add the mushrooms and green onions and sauté until tender. Remove from heat.
2. Blend mushrooms, onions, and remaining filling ingredients together.
3. Spoon mixture into dumpling wrappers and pinch closed.
4. Cook dumplings.
   a. To fry dumplings, preheat oil in a wok for 30 seconds on high heat, then lower heat to medium. Cook dumplings on each side for about 3 minutes or until golden brown.

b. To steam dumplings, place in a steamer basket or on an elevated plate in a wok over water on high heat for about 10 minutes.
5. Serve hot.

Cheesy Breakfast Dumplings

Kickstarter backer Dan Kinder requested this great breakfast dumpling. Even though it calls for ground turkey sausage, you can easily make this a vegetarian dumpling by removing the turkey and doubling the amount of potatoes.

- ½ cup shredded potato (frozen is fine)
- ¼ cup ground turkey sausage
- ¼ cup mushrooms, chopped
- ¼ cup butter, melted
- 2 Tbsp milk
- ¼ cup cheese, shredded
- 2 Tbsp green onion, chopped
- 1 egg, whisked
- Dash of salt
- Dash of pepper
- Dash of garlic powder
- 12 dumpling wrappers
- 1 cup of oil
- Salsa for dipping (recipe in the Sauces section)

1. Mix all filling ingredients together.
2. Spoon mixture into dumpling wrappers and pinch closed.
3. To fry dumplings, preheat oil in a wok for 30 seconds on high

heat, then lower heat to medium. Cook dumplings on each side for about 3 minutes or until golden brown.

4. Always cut a dumpling open to make sure it is cooked through.
5. Serve hot with Salsa for dipping.

Crazy Dumplings

Cheesy Potato Crawfish Dumplings

This delicious crawfish dumpling is sure to remind you of the taste of New Orleans!

- 1 Tbsp oil
- ½ cup crawfish meat
- ¼ cup onion, chopped
- ¼ cup celery, chopped
- 1 garlic clove, pressed
- ¼ cup potato, boiled and chopped
- ¼ cup cheese, shredded
- 1 green onion, chopped
- 1 Tbsp sour cream
- 1 Tbsp Cajun seasoning
- Dash of hot sauce
- Dash of salt
- Dash of pepper
- 12 dumpling wrappers
- 1 cup of oil

1. In a wok, heat oil. Add crawfish meat, onion, celery, and garlic. Sauté until meat is cooked and veggies are tender. Remove from heat.

2. Blend crayfish mixture together with remaining filling ingredients.
3. Spoon mixture into dumpling wrappers and pinch closed.
4. To fry dumplings, preheat oil in a wok for 30 seconds on high heat, then lower heat to medium. Cook dumplings on each side for about 3 minutes or until golden brown.
5. Always cut a dumpling open to make sure it is cooked through.

Crazy Dumplings

Chicken, Corn, and Cilantro Dumplings

Chicken, corn, and cilantro are ingredients you can find all over China and in a wide variety of dishes, but I had never seen them combined into a dumpling before. It resulted in a perfect blend.

- 1 cup chicken, chopped
- ¼ cup red bell pepper, deseeded and chopped
- ¼ cup corn kernels
- 1 tsp ground cumin
- ¼ cup cilantro, chopped
- ¼ cup mozzarella cheese, shredded
- 1 garlic clove, pressed
- Dash of salt
- Dash of pepper
- 12 dumpling wrappers
- 1 cup of oil

1. In a bowl, mix together all of the filling ingredients.
2. Spoon mixture into dumpling wrappers and pinch closed.
3. Cook dumplings.
    a. To fry dumplings, preheat oil in a wok for 30 seconds on high heat, then lower heat to medium. Cook dumplings on each side for about 3 minutes or until golden brown.

b. To steam dumplings, place in a steamer basket or on an elevated plate in a wok over water on high heat for about 10 minutes.

c. To boil dumplings, place in boiling water for about 10 minutes.

4. Always cut a dumpling open to make sure it is cooked through.

Chicken Enchilada Dumplings

If you read the first Crazy Dumplings cookbook, you know that I love Mexican food! It's one of the things I miss most here in China. So I had to include a couple of Mexican-inspired dumplings in this book.

- ½ cup cooked chicken, shredded
- ¼ cup cream cheese
- ¼ cup sharp cheddar cheese, shredded
- ¼ cup canned green chilies
- ¼ cup onion, chopped
- 1 jalapeno pepper, chopped, seeds and ribs removed for less heat
- 1 Tbsp cayenne pepper
- 1 Tbsp chili powder
- 1 Tbsp cumin
- 1 garlic clove, pressed
- 12 dumpling wrappers
- 1 cup of oil
- Salsa or Avocado Lime Sauce (recipes in the Sauces section) for dipping

1. In a bowl, blend all of the filling ingredients together.
2. Spoon mixture into dumpling wrappers and pinch closed.

3. To fry dumplings, preheat oil in a wok for 30 seconds on high heat, then lower heat to medium. Cook dumplings on each side for about 3 minutes or until golden brown.
4. Serve hot with Salsa or Avocado Lime Sauce for dipping

Crazy Dumplings

Chinese Veggie Dumplings

I wish I could have come up with a better name for this dumpling, but it delivers what it promises. This easy dumpling is sure to please the herbivores and carnivores in your life.

- 1 Tbsp sesame oil
- 1 tsp ginger, microplaned
- 1 cup mushrooms, chopped
- ¼ cup carrot, chopped
- ¼ cup cabbage, chopped
- ¼ cup celery, chopped
- 2 green onions, chopped
- 1 tsp Chinese Five-Spice Powder
- 1 Tbsp cornstarch mixed with 1 Tbsp water
- 12 dumpling wrappers
- 1 cup of oil, if frying
- Chinese Chili Sauce or Thai Sweet Chili Sauce for dipping (recipes in the Sauces section)

1. In a wok, heat sesame oil. Add ginger and sauté until fragrant. Add remaining filling ingredients except the cornstarch slurry and stir-fry until all ingredients are cooked through.
2. Add cornstarch slurry and mix until ingredients start to stick together.

3. Remove from heat. Once the mixture is cool enough to handle, spoon it into dumpling wrappers and pinch closed.
4. Cook dumplings
   a. To fry dumplings, preheat oil in a wok for 30 seconds on high heat, then lower heat to medium. Cook dumplings on each side for about 3 minutes or until golden brown.
   b. To steam dumplings, place in a steamer basket or on an elevated plate in a wok over water **on high heat** for about 10 minutes.
   c. To boil dumplings, place in boiling water for about 10 minutes.
5. Serve hot with favorite sauce for dipping.

Crazy Dumplings

Chorizo Breakfast Dumplings

Kickstarter backer Chris Edwards requested a dumpling recipe with a runny egg at the end. At first, I wasn't sure it could be done because of how dumplings are cooked, but I think this is exactly what he was looking for. This dumpling requires very little cooking, so you could simply flash fry it or steam it just enough to cook the dumpling wrapper without heating the egg yolks solid. Note the shorter cooking times at the end of the recipe.

- 1 Tbsp oil
- ½ cup chorizo, crumbled
- ¼ cup avocado, chopped
- ¼ cup tomato, chopped
- ¼ cup mozzarella cheese, shredded
- 2 egg yolks
- 12 dumpling wrappers
- 1 cup of oil
- Chipotle Mayonnaise for dipping (recipe in the Sauces section)

1. In a wok, heat oil. Add chorizo and sauté until cooked through. Remove from heat.
2. In a bowl, blend cooked chorizo with avocado, tomato, and mozzarella cheese. Set aside.
3. Whisk egg yolks. Blend egg yolks with chorizo mixture.

4. Spoon mixture into dumpling wrappers and pinch closed.
5. Cook dumplings.
   a. To fry dumplings, preheat oil in a wok for 30 seconds on high heat, then lower heat to medium. Cook dumplings on each side for about 1 minute or until golden brown.
   b. To steam dumplings, place in a steamer basket or on an elevated plate in a wok over water on high heat for about 10 minutes.
6. Serve hot with Chipotle Mayonnaise for dipping.

Citrus-Herb Salmon Dumplings

This lovely dumpling is sophisticated and flavorful. Since it is a fish dish, it is one of the few that also works steamed for a lighter dish. A perfect addition to your dumpling party!

- 1 cup salmon meat, chopped
- Juice of 1 lemon
- 1 Tbsp orange juice
- 6 black olives, chopped
- 1 Tbsp dried basil
- 1 Tbsp dried thyme
- Dash of salt
- 12 dumpling wrappers
- 1 cup of oil, if frying

1. Mix all ingredients together.
2. Spoon mixture into dumpling wrappers and pinch closed.
3. Cook dumplings.
   a. To fry dumplings, preheat oil in a wok for 30 seconds on high heat, then lower heat to medium. Cook dumplings on each side for about 3 minutes or until golden brown.

    b. To steam dumplings, place in a steamer basket or on an elevated plate in a wok over water on high heat for about 10 minutes.
4. Always cut a dumpling open to make sure it is cooked through.

Crazy Dumplings

Coconut Lime Chicken Dumplings

You put the lime in the dumpling and you eat it all up! You know you just sang that. This Thai favorite served in a dumpling wrapper will have your taste buds singing too!

- Juice and zest of 2 limes
- ¼ cup cilantro, chopped
- 2 lemongrass stalks, chopped
- 1 tsp oil
- 1 cup coconut milk
- 1 cup chicken breast, chopped
- 3 tablespoons Nuoc Cham (Available in the Sauces section)
- 1 Tbsp soy sauce
- 12 dumpling wrappers
- 1 cup of oil

1. In a blender, add the lime zest, cilantro, and lemongrass. Blend to a smooth paste.
2. Heat **1 tsp of** oil in a wok over a high heat. Add the paste and fry for 1-2 minutes until it is aromatic. Add the coconut milk and mix.
3. Turn heat to low and **add the chicken.** Sauté until chicken is cooked through.
4. Add the **Nuoc Cham** and soy sauce and simmer for a further 5 minutes.

5. Pour in the lime juice and mix well.
6. Drain the chicken from the sauce and reserve the sauce.
7. Let the chicken cool enough to handle.
8. Spoon chicken into dumpling wrappers and pinch closed.
9. To fry dumplings, preheat oil in a wok for 30 seconds on high heat, then lower heat to medium. Cook dumplings on each side for about 3 minutes or until golden brown.
10. Serve hot with reserved coconut lime sauce for dipping.

Cola Chinese Chicken Dumplings

I have no idea where this recipe originated, but Cola chicken has quickly become popular throughout Asia. Using American soda to make Chinese chicken is already a pretty crazy combination, which made it a perfect concoction for Crazy Dumplings!

- 1 Tbsp oil
- 3 garlic cloves, pressed
- 1 tsp fresh ginger, microplaned
- 3 red chili peppers, chopped (more or less depending on heat level desired)
- 1 can of cola
- ¼ cup soy sauce
- 2 Tbsp Shaoxing wine
- 1 cup chicken, diced
- 12 dumpling wrappers
- 1 cup of oil

1. In a wok, heat 1 Tbsp oil. Add garlic, ginger, and chili peppers and sauté until fragrant.
2. Add the cola, soy sauce, and wine and bring to a simmer.
3. Add chicken and cook through, allowing the sauce to reduce. Lower heat if needed to prevent the sauce from burning as it thickens. The sauce should turn into a thick

glaze after about 10 minutes.

4. Remove from heat and drain the chicken from the sauce, reserving the sauce. Once the chicken is cool enough to handle, spoon chicken into dumpling wrappers and pinch closed.
5. To fry dumplings, preheat oil in a wok for 30 seconds on high heat, then lower heat to medium. Cook dumplings on each side for about 3 minutes or until golden brown.
6. Serve hot with reserved cola sauce for dipping.

Creamed Spinach with Pork Dumplings

This very interesting dumpling was inspired by Kickstarter backer Týna Dvořáková's mother's Czech creamed spinach recipe. I had to take a few liberties here, as I'm not very familiar with Czech food – and of course no one can cook quite like your mom – but hopefully this fun take on a family tradition would meet with her mom's approval. Týna wanted to dedicate this recipe to, "my brother Jirka, who introduced me to jiaozi, and my mum Eva, who taught me how to cook."

- 1 Tbsp butter
- 5 garlic cloves, pressed
- 1 cups fresh spinach, chopped
- Dash of salt
- Dash of pepper
- ¼ cup cream
- ½ cup ground pork, browned
- 12 dumpling wrappers
- 1 cup of oil

1. In a wok, heat butter. Add garlic and sauté until fragrant.
2. Add the spinach, salt, and pepper. Sauté for about 5 minutes, letting the spinach wilt down and all water that the spinach releases is cooked away. Add the cream and blend into a smooth sauce.

3. Add the cooked ground pork and heat through. Drain the pork from the mixture and reserve the spinach sauce.
4. Let the pork cool enough to handle.
5. Spoon pork into dumpling wrappers and pinch closed.
6. To fry dumplings, preheat oil in a wok for 30 seconds on high heat, then lower heat to medium. Cook dumplings on each side for about 3 minutes or until golden brown.
7. Serve hot with reserved spinach sauce for dipping

Creamy Tuna Dumplings

This is a fun and fancy way to dress up a tuna sandwich. Your kids are sure to love them!

- 1 Tbsp oil
- ¼ cup onion, chopped
- 1 clove garlic, pressed
- 1 can of tuna, 6 oz., drained
- ¼ cup cream cheese
- ¼ cup mozzarella cheese, shredded
- 2 Tbsp black olives, chopped
- 1 tsp dill
- 12 dumpling wrappers
- 1 cup of oil, if frying

1. In a wok, heat oil. Add onion and garlic. Sauté until onion is tender. Remove from heat and then blend with tuna, cream cheese, mozzarella cheese, olives, and dill.
2. Spoon mixture into dumpling wrappers and pinch closed.
3. To fry dumplings, preheat oil in a wok for 30 seconds on high heat, then lower heat to medium. Cook dumplings on each side for about 3 minutes or until golden brown.
4. Serve hot.

Amanda Roberts

Delicious Turkey Dumplings

The seasonings in this dumpling are strong enough to pair with ground turkey meat, which is more healthy than most other meats but sometimes rather bland. Pair these with the Honey Chipotle Sauce in the Sauces section to really kick up the flavor.

- 1 Tbsp oil
- 1 cup ground turkey
- ¼ cup tomato, chopped
- ¼ cup onion, chopped
- 1 clove of garlic, pressed
- Dash of pepper
- Dash of chicken bouillon
- ¼ cup fresh cilantro, chopped
- 12 dumpling wrappers
- 1 cup of oil, if frying
- Honey Chipotle Sauce for dipping (recipe in the Sauces section)

1. In a wok, heat the oil. Add turkey, tomato, onion, garlic, pepper, and chicken bouillon. Sauté until turkey is no longer pink. Remove from heat and blend in cilantro. Let mixture cool enough for handling.
2. Spoon mixture into dumpling wrappers and pinch closed.

Crazy Dumplings

3. Cook dumplings.

    a. To fry dumplings, preheat oil in a wok for 30 seconds on high heat, then lower heat to medium. Cook dumplings on each side for about 3 minutes or until golden brown.

    b. To steam dumplings, place in a steamer basket or on an elevated plate in a wok over water on high heat for about 10 minutes.

    c. To boil dumplings, place in boiling water for about 10 minutes.

4. Always cut a dumpling open to make sure it is cooked through.

5. Serve hot with Honey Chipotle Sauce for dipping.

Amanda Roberts

Easy Chinese Chicken Dumplings

You can find many different dumpling recipes all around China. While many tend to be made with pork, chicken dumplings are popular around Chinese New Year. This is a simple yet delicious recipe you can try the next time CNY rolls around.

- 1 cup chicken, chopped
- ¼ cup carrot, chopped
- ¼ cup cabbage, chopped
- 1 tsp ginger, microplaned
- 1 Tbsp soy sauce
- 1 Tbsp sesame oil
- 1 green onion, chopped
- 12 dumpling wrappers
- 1 cup of oil, if frying
- Chinese Chili Sauce or Thai Sweet Chili sauce for dipping (recipes in the Sauces section)

1. In a bowl, add all the filling ingredients and mix well.
2. Spoon mixture into dumpling wrappers and pinch closed.
3. Cook dumplings.
    a. To fry dumplings, preheat oil in a wok for 30 seconds on high heat, then lower heat to medium. Cook dumplings on each side for about 3 minutes or until golden brown.

Crazy Dumplings

    b. To steam dumplings, place in a steamer basket or on an elevated plate in a wok over water on high heat for about 10 minutes.

    c. To boil dumplings, place in boiling water for about 10 minutes.

4. Always cut a dumpling open to make sure it is cooked through.
5. Serve hot with choice of sauce for dipping.

Amanda Roberts

Egg and Mushroom Wonton Soup

Use the Traditional Dumpling Filling recipe from the beginning of the Savory Dumplings chapter to make traditional Wonton Soup or you can use this fun new twist on wontons for a yummy new soup. Shitake mushrooms are really nice in this soup, but you can use whatever mushrooms you like.

- 2 Tbsp oil, divided
- ½ cup mushrooms, chopped
- 2 eggs
- 1 Tbsp oyster sauce
- ½ Tbsp Cornstarch mixed in ½ Tbsp water
- 5 green onions, chopped, divided
- 12 dumpling wrappers
- 1 garlic clove, pressed
- 1 Tbsp ginger, microplaned
- 10 cups chicken broth

1. In a wok, heat 1 Tbsp oil. Add the mushrooms and sauté until shriveled. Add eggs, oyster sauce, cornstarch slurry, and 1 chopped green onion. Scramble egg mixture.
2. Remove from heat. When scrambled egg mixture is cool enough to handle, spoon mixture into dumpling wrappers and pinch closed. Set dumplings aside.

Crazy Dumplings

3. In a pot, heat 1 Tbsp oil. Add garlic and ginger and sauté until fragrant. Add half of the remaining green onions and all the chicken broth and bring to a boil. Reduce heat and let the broth simmer for about 20 minutes.
4. Increase heat so the broth returns to a boil. Slowly (preferably with a slotted spoon to prevent splashing) add in the dumplings. Stir gently until the wontons are cooked through, about 10 minutes.
5. Serve hot, sprinkled with remaining green onions.

Amanda Roberts

Eggplant Ricotta Dumplings

I don't think I ever ate eggplant before I moved to China, but now it is one of my favorite foods. This versatile veggie is a great staple for vegetarian dishes like this one.

- ¼ cup fresh basil, chopped
- 2 Tbsp roasted pine nuts
- ½ cup ricotta cheese
- 1 tsp Italian seasoning
- 1 tsp garlic powder
- Dash of salt
- Dash of pepper
- 1 Tbsp oil
- ½ cup eggplant, thinly sliced
- 12 dumpling wrappers
- 1 cup oil (if frying)
- Porcupine Dipping Sauce (recipe in the Sauces section)

1. In a bowl, combine basil pine nuts, ricotta cheese, and seasonings. Blend well and set aside.
2. In a wok, heat 1 Tbsp oil. Add the eggplant slices. Apply pressure to the eggplant to release moisture, flipping occasionally. Remove eggplant slices when tender.

Crazy Dumplings

3. Cut eggplant into small pieces and stir into ricotta cheese mixture.
4. Spoon mixture into dumpling wrappers and pinch closed.
5. Cook dumplings.
    a. To fry dumplings, preheat oil in a wok for 30 seconds on high heat, then lower heat to medium. Cook dumplings on each side for about 3 minutes or until golden brown.
    b. To steam dumplings, place in a steamer basket or on an elevated plate in a wok over water on high heat for about 10 minutes.
    c. To boil dumplings, place in boiling water for about 10 minutes.
6. Serve hot with Porcupine Dipping Sauce.

Amanda Roberts

Eggs Benedict Dumplings

This is similar to a vegetarian breakfast quiche you can easily stuff into dumpling wrappers for a fun dumpling breakfast.

- Dumplings:
- 1 Tbsp butter
- 1 cup fresh baby spinach leaves
- Juice of 2 lemons
- 2 Large eggs
- 1 Tbsp honey
- 12 dumpling wrappers
- 1 cup of oil
- Hollandaise Sauce:
- 2 egg yolks
- Juice of 1 lemon
- Dash of salt
- Dash of cayenne pepper
- 5 Tbsp butter

To make the dumplings:
1. Melt butter in a wok. Sauté spinach with juice from 1 lemon.
2. Whisk eggs, honey, and juice of the other lemon together.

Crazy Dumplings

Blend with sautéed spinach.

3. Spoon mixture into dumpling wrappers and pinch closed.
4. To fry dumplings, preheat oil in a wok for 30 seconds on high heat, then lower heat to medium. Cook dumplings on each side for about 3 minutes or until golden brown.
5. Always cut a dumpling open to make sure it is cooked through.

To make the hollandaise sauce:

1. Whisk together egg yolks, lemon juice, salt and cayenne pepper. Set aside.
2. Melt butter in a saucepan. Do not let it boil. Remove from heat.
3. Slowly drizzle egg mixture into the butter, whisking all the while.
4. Serve dumplings hot, drizzled with hollandaise sauce.

Amanda Roberts

Firecracker Chicken Dumplings

These dumplings are inspired by one of my favorite appetizers at a certain American steakhouse. They aren't exactly the same, but they are creamy, spicy, and cheesy! It goes lovely with the Avocado Lime Sauce in the Sauces section.

- ¼ cup Sriracha sauce
- 1 Tbsp butter, melted
- 1 tsp garlic powder
- Dash of cayenne pepper
- 1 tsp cornstarch blended with 1 tsp water
- 1 cup cooked chicken, chopped
- ¼ cup cheddar cheese, shredded
- 12 dumpling wrappers
- 1 cup of oil
- Avocado Lime Sauce for dipping (recipe in the sauces section)

1. In a bowl, whisk together hot sauce, butter, powder, garlic powder, and cornstarch slurry.
2. Blend sauce together with chicken and cheese.
3. Spoon mixture into dumpling wrappers and pinch closed.

Crazy Dumplings

4. To fry dumplings, preheat oil in a wok for 30 seconds on high heat, then lower heat to medium. Cook dumplings on each side for about 3 minutes or until golden brown.
5. Serve hot with Avocado Lime Sauce for dipping.

Amanda Roberts

Fresh Spring Chicken Dumplings

This is another dumpling that is light, healthy, and flavorful. The fresh corn gives it a sweet hint. Feel free to steam this one as well for a summer dinner or snack. The wine is for flavor and to help the ingredients meld together. If your chicken is very juicy and you are worried ¼ of a cup of wine might be too much, just add it bit by bit until you are comfortable with the consistency.

- ½ cup cooked chicken, chopped
- ¼ cup fresh corn kernels
- ¼ cup onion, chopped
- ¼ cup fresh peas
- ¼ cup sparkling white wine
- 1 Tbsp dill
- Dash of salt
- Dash of pepper
- 12 dumpling wrappers
- 1 cup of oil, if frying

1. Mix all dumpling ingredients together.
2. Spoon mixture into dumpling wrappers and pinch closed.
3. Cook dumplings.
    a. To fry dumplings, preheat oil in a wok for 30 seconds on high heat, then lower heat to medium. Cook dumplings on each side for about 3 minutes or until golden brown.

    b. To steam dumplings, place in a steamer basket or on an elevated plate in a wok over water on high heat for about 10 minutes.

4. Serve hot.

Amanda Roberts

Fried Pickle Dumplings

My BFF Cherith and I are obsessed with fried pickles. So this fried pickle dumpling recipe is for her! Use your favorite cheese to make it your own!

- ¾ cup dill pickles, chopped
- ¼ cup cheese, shredded
- 1 Tbsp chipotle powder
- 1 tsp garlic powder
- 1 tsp paprika
- 12 dumpling wrappers
- 1 cup of oil, if frying
- Chipotle Mayonnaise for dipping (recipe in the Sauces section)

1. Mix all filling ingredients together.
2. Spoon mixture into dumpling wrappers and pinch closed.
3. To fry dumplings, preheat oil in a wok for 30 seconds on high heat, then lower heat to medium. Cook dumplings on each side for about 3 minutes or until golden brown.
4. Serve hot with Chipotle Mayonnaise for dipping.

Crazy Dumplings

Guacamole Dumplings

I know I'm about to blow your mind, but even guacamole can be a dumpling filling!

- 2 ripe avocados
- 1 tomato, peeled, seeded, chopped
- ¼ cup onion, chopped
- Juice of 1 lime
- 1 garlic clove, pressed
- 2 Tbsp fresh cilantro, chopped (or as much as you want. I like a LOT!)
- 12 dumpling wrappers
- 1 cup of oil for frying
- Salsa for dipping (recipe in the Sauces section)

1. Slice open avocados and spoon out meat. Mash the avocado meat with a fork.
2. Add in remaining filling ingredients and blend thoroughly.
3. To fry dumplings, preheat oil in a wok for 30 seconds on high heat, then lower heat to medium. Cook dumplings on each side for about 3 minutes or until golden brown.

4. Always cut a dumpling open to make sure it is cooked through.
5. Serve hot with Salsa for dipping.

General Tsao's Dumplings

How General Tsao came to be associated with his namesake chicken dish is a bit of a mystery. But there is no mystery that this will certainly become one of your favorite dumplings!

- 2 Tbsp cornstarch blended with 2 Tbsp water
- ½ cup sugar
- ¼ cup soy sauce
- 2 Tbsp vinegar
- 2 Tbsp Shaoxing wine
- ½ cup chicken broth
- 1 Tbsp oil
- 1 cup chicken, chopped
- 1 garlic clove, pressed
- 3 small red chilies, chopped
- 2 green onions, chopped
- 12 dumpling wrappers
- 1 cup of oil, if frying

1. In a bowl, whisk together cornstarch slurry, sugar, soy sauce, vinegar, wine, and chicken broth. Set aside.
2. In a wok, heat oil. Add chicken, garlic, chilies, and chicken broth sauce. Sauté until chicken is cooked. Remove from heat and toss with green onions.
3. Drain sauce from chicken and reserve. Let chicken cool enough to handle.
4. Spoon chicken mixture into dumpling wrappers and pinch closed.
5. To fry dumplings, preheat oil in a wok for 30 seconds on high heat, then lower heat to medium. Cook dumplings on each side for about 3 minutes or until golden brown.
6. Always cut a dumpling open to make sure it is cooked through.
7. Serve hot with excess sauce for dipping or drizzle sauce over dumplings before serving.

Grilled Cheese Tomato Soup Dumplings

This dumpling is so easy to make, yet I guarantee people will be asking, "How did you do that?!?" if you serve it for your friends and family. Don't worry, it's our little secret. Use your favorite cheese to make this dumpling all your own.

- 1 cup cheese, shredded
- ½ can condensed tomato soup
- 12 dumpling wrappers
- 1 cup of oil, if frying

1. In a bowl, combine cheese and soup.
2. Spoon cheese mixture into dumpling wrappers and pinch closed.
3. To fry dumplings, preheat oil in a wok for 30 seconds on high heat, then lower heat to medium. Cook dumplings on each side for about 3 minutes or until golden brown.
4. Serve hot, but be careful when eating in case soup oozes out.

Amanda Roberts

Ham and Honey Mustard Dumplings

These dumplings are very easy to make, but are full of flavor. These would make a great afterschool snack or light weekend lunch.

- ½ cup mayonnaise
- 2 Tbsp yellow mustard
- 2 Tbsp honey
- ½ tsp lemon juice
- 1 cup ham, chopped
- ¼ cup raisins
- 12 dumpling wrappers
- 1 cup of oil for frying

1. In a bowl, mix mayonnaise, mustard, honey, and lemon juice. Set aside.
2. Blend 2 Tbsp of the honey mustard mix, the ham, and the raisins.
3. Spoon ham mixture into dumpling wrappers and pinch closed.
4. To fry dumplings, preheat oil in a wok for 30 seconds on high heat, then lower heat to medium. Cook dumplings on each side for about 3 minutes or until golden brown.

Crazy Dumplings

5. Serve hot with remaining honey mustard sauce for dipping.

Amanda Roberts

Honey Pepper Salmon Dumplings

This flavorful recipe is sweet with a kick of pepper. Sure to be your new favorite! You can use fresh, canned, or leftover salmon.

- ¾ cup honey
- ¼ cup soy sauce
- ¼ cup brown sugar
- ¼ cup pineapple juice
- Juice of 1 lemon
- 2 Tbsp olive oil
- 1 tsp black pepper
- 1 tsp cayenne pepper
- Dash of paprika
- Dash of garlic powder
- 1 cup cooked salmon, chopped
- 12 dumpling wrappers
- 1 cup of oil, if frying

1. In a saucepan, add all filling ingredients except salmon and heat over medium heat. Stir occasionally until sauce begins to boil. Simmer uncovered for 15 minutes until syrupy.
2. Remove from heat and blend in salmon.

Crazy Dumplings

3. Drain sauce from salmon and reserve.
4. Spoon salmon mixture into dumpling wrappers and pinch closed.
5. Cook dumplings.

    a. To fry dumplings, preheat oil in a wok for 30 seconds on high heat, then lower heat to medium. Cook dumplings on each side for about 3 minutes or until golden brown.

    b. To steam dumplings, place in a steamer basket or on an elevated plate in a wok over water on high heat for about 10 minutes.

6. Always cut a dumpling open to make sure it is cooked through.
7. Serve hot with reserved sauce for dipping.

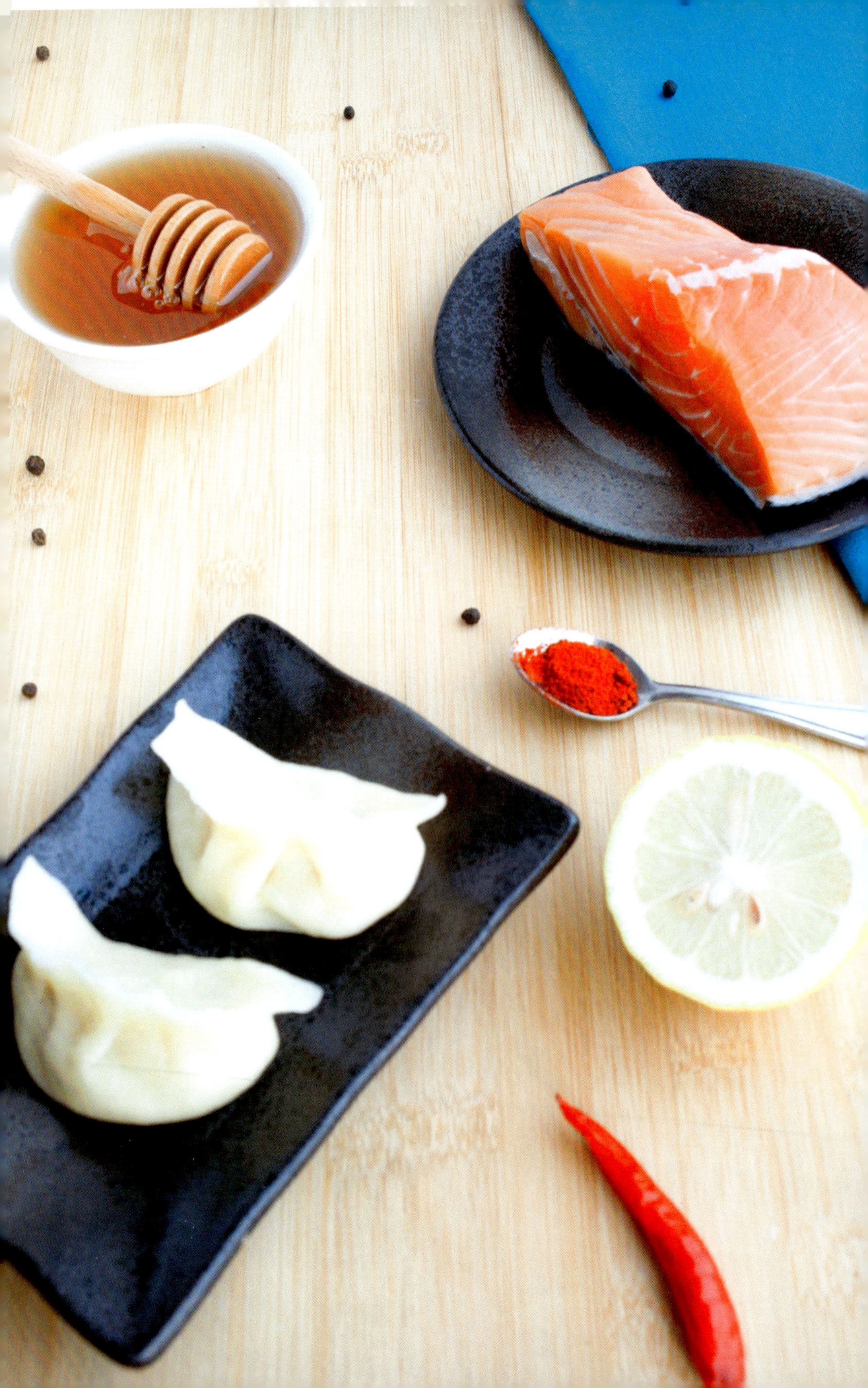

Crazy Dumplings

Hummus, Crab, and Jalapeno Dumplings

Hummus is so versatile, it can be way more than a dip! I've thought about writing a Crazy Hummus book to show just all the wonderful things you can do with hummus. What do you think?

- ½ cup hummus
- ½ cup crab meat, chopped
- ¼ cup mozzarella cheese, shredded
- ¼ cup jalapenos, chopped (seeds and ribs removed for less heat)
- ¼ cup tomato, chopped
- 1 green onion, chopped
- Dash of salt
- Dash of pepper
- 12 dumpling wrappers
- 1 cup of oil, if frying

1. In a bowl, mix all filling ingredients together.
2. Spoon mixture into dumpling wrappers and pinch closed.
3. Cook dumplings.
    a. To fry dumplings, preheat oil in a wok for 30 seconds on high heat, then lower heat to medium. Cook dumplings on each side for about 3 minutes or until golden brown.

b. To steam dumplings, place in a steamer basket or on an elevated plate in a wok over water on high heat for about 10 minutes.

4. Always cut a dumpling open to make sure it is cooked through.

Jalapeño Chicken Dumplings

This creamy, spicy chicken dumpling is easy to make, but sure to delight! I paired it with the Thai Sweet Chili Sauce to temper the heat of the jalapenos.

- ½ cup cooked chicken, chopped
- ¼ cup cream cheese
- ¼ cup jalapenos, chopped (seed and ribs removed for less heat)
- 1 tsp garlic powder
- 1 tsp cumin powder
- ¼ cup sharp cheddar cheese
- 12 dumpling wrappers
- 1 cup of oil
- Thai Sweet Chili Sauce for dipping (recipe in Sauces section)

1. In a bowl, blend together all filling ingredients.
2. Spoon mixture into dumpling wrappers and pinch closed.
3. To fry dumplings, preheat oil in a wok for 30 seconds on high heat, then lower heat to medium. Cook dumplings on each side for about 3 minutes or until golden brown.

4. Always cut a dumpling open to make sure it is cooked through.
5. Serve hot with Thai Sweet Chili Sauce for dipping.

Kimchee Bokkeumbap Dumplings

Kickstarter backer Michael Kroeker requested a kimchee bokkeumbap inspired dumpling. A Kimchee dumpling would be quite easy, simply fill a dumpling wrapper with delicious kimchee and fry! That's not Crazy enough for me, so I was excited to see a request for a dumpling that was a new twist on this popular Korean dish. It's just crazy enough for this book!

- ¼ cup kimchee (see Step 1 below)
- 2 Tbsp kimchee juice
- 1 tsp gochujang (Korean hot pepper paste)
- 1 tsp soy sauce
- 2 tsp sesame oil
- 1 cup steamed rice
- 1 Tbsp Vegetable oil
- 1 green onion, chopped
- 12 dumpling wrappers
- 1 cup of oil, if frying

1. Squeeze out as much kimchee juice as possible from the kimchee. Reserve 2 Tbsp of the juice. Then measure out ¼ cup of kimchee and chop.
2. Whisk the kimchee juice, gochujang and soy sauce together until the gochujang is completely dissolved.

3. Drizzle the sesame oil on the rice and stir to break up any big clumps.
4. Put the vegetable oil in a frying pan and heat over medium heat until hot. Add the chopped kimchee and stir-fry until the kimchee starts to brown and is very fragrant.
5. Add the rice and stir-fry with a spatula, pressing down on any clumps until the rice is uniform in color.
6. Pour the kimchee juice mixture over the rice, and turn up the heat to high. Stir-fry, tossing the rice occasionally until the rice starts to brown and doesn't stick together quite as much.
7. When the fried rice is done, set it aside to cool.
8. When the rice is cool enough to handle, spoon the mixture into the dumpling wrappers and pinch closed.
9. To fry dumplings, preheat oil in a wok for 30 seconds on high heat, then lower heat to medium. Cook dumplings on each side for about 3 minutes or until golden brown.
10. Serve hot with extra kimchee, a fried egg on the side, and soy sauce for dipping.

Crazy Dumplings

Korean Fried Chicken (KFC) Dumplings

Kickstarter backer David Spaxman requested a Korean fried chicken dumpling. This sweet and spicy dumpling is sure to become your new favorite!

- 3 Tbsp brown sugar
- 1 Tbsp gochujang (Korean sweet chili paste)
- 1 Tbsp gochugaru (Korean hot pepper paste, use more or less depending on heat level desired)
- 1 Tbsp soy sauce
- ¼ cup soju (Korean liquor, if you can't find it, Chinese baijiu or vodka will work)
- 3 garlic cloves, pressed
- 2 tsp ginger, microplaned
- 1 tsp   sesame oil
- 1 cup chicken, chopped
- 1 Tbsp cornstarch
- ½ cup oil
- 12 dumpling wrappers
- 1 cup of oil, if frying

1. In a saucepan, combine brown sugar, gochujang, soy sauce, soji, garlic, ginger, and sesame oil. Boil until the sauce thickens. Remove from heat and set aside.
2. Toss the chicken in the cornstarch to coat.

3. Heat the ½ cup of oil in a wok. Carefully add chicken to fry. Turn to brown evenly. Remove from oil and blot with paper towels to remove excess oil.
4. Toss the chicken with the sauce to coat. Remove chicken from sauce and reserve sauce.
5. Spoon chicken into dumpling wrappers and pinch closed.
6. To fry dumplings, preheat oil in a wok for 30 seconds on high heat, then lower heat to medium. Cook dumplings on each side for about 3 minutes or until golden brown.
7. Serve hot with extra sauce for dipping.

Lamb with Pomegranate Salsa Dumplings

This dumpling is for Kickstarter backer Kyle Klems. I wish I had used this one for the photos for the book. It is just beautiful to look at!

- 1 Tbsp oil
- 1 cup ground lamb meat
- Dash of salt
- Dash of pepper
- 1 garlic clove, pressed
- 2 Tbsp red cooking wine
- 1 pomegranate, seeded
- 1 small apple, chopped
- 1 jalapeno, chopped (seeds and ribs removed for less heat)
- ¼ cup cilantro, chopped
- 1 Tbsp olive oil
- 1 Tbsp balsamic vinegar
- Juice of 1 lime
- 12 dumpling wrappers
- 1 cup of oil, if frying

1. In a wok, heat oil. Add lamb, salt, pepper, garlic, and cooking

wine. Brown meat. Remove from heat.

2. In a bowl, mix together pomegranate, apple, jalapeno, cilantro, olive oil, vinegar, and lime juice.
3. Mix meat and 2 Tbsp of salsa together.
4. Spoon mixture into dumpling wrappers and pinch closed.
5. To fry dumplings, preheat oil in a wok for 30 seconds on high heat, then lower heat to medium. Cook dumplings on each side for about 3 minutes or until golden brown.
6. Serve hot with extra Pomegranate Salsa for dipping.

Lobster Cream Cheese Dumplings

What's great about dumplings is that they are appropriate for any occasion. Dinner for one, big party, wedding reception, holiday meal – no matter how casual or fancy, you can find a dumpling for the occasion. This is one that would be great to pull out for a more upscale affair, yet is still easy to make.

- ½ cup cream cheese
- 1 green onion, chopped
- 1 tsp Sriracha sauce
- ½ cup lobster meat, chopped
- 12 dumpling wrappers
- 1 cup of oil
- Thai Sweet Chili Sauce (recipe in the Sauces section) for dipping

1. In a bowl, blend cream cheese, green onion, and Sriracha sauce. Add lobster meat and mix well.
2. Spoon mixture into dumpling wrappers and pinch closed.
3. To fry dumplings, preheat oil in a wok for 30 seconds on high heat, then lower heat to medium. Cook dumplings on each side for about 3 minutes or until golden brown.

4. Serve hot with Thai Sweet Chili Sauce for dipping.

Crazy Dumplings

🧀 Macaroni and Cheese Dumplings 🧀

You can, of course, simply use prepared box mac and cheese as the filling for this recipe, but a box will render much more filling than you need for 12 dumplings. This homemade recipe should give you just what you need with a lot more flavor and help you eat outside the box.

- ½ cup small pasta
- ¼ cup sharp cheddar cheese, shredded
- ¼ cup cream cheese
- 2 Tbsp milk
- 1 tsp garlic powder
- 1 tsp chili powder
- 1 tsp black pepper
- 12 dumpling wrappers
- 1 cup of oil, if frying

1. In a bowl, mix cheddar cheese, cream cheese, milk, and spices together. Set aside.
2. Prepare pasta according to package directions.
3. While pasta is still hot, blend with cheese mixture.
4. Spoon mixture into dumpling wrappers and pinch closed.

5. To fry dumplings, preheat oil in a wok for 30 seconds on high heat, then lower heat to medium. Cook dumplings on each side for about 3 minutes or until golden brown.
6. Serve hot.

Crazy Dumplings

Nepali Momos

Momos are one of the most popular dishes in Nepal. Like dumplings, there are many ways to prepare momos, but this recipe will give you a taste of the Himalayas.

- 1 cup lean ground lamb or pork
- ½ cup red onion, chopped
- 2 green onions, chopped
- 2 Tbsp cilantro, chopped
- 1 red chili, chopped
- 2 garlic cloves, pressed
- 1 Tbsp curry powder
- 1 tsp fresh ginger, microplaned
- 1 tsp Sichuan peppercorns
- 1 tsp nutmeg powder
- 1 tsp turmeric
- Dash of salt
- 12 dumpling wrappers
- 1 cup of oil, if frying
- Chinese Chili Sauce or Thai Sweet Chili Sauce for dipping (recipe in Sauces section)

1. In a bowl, mix all filling ingredients together. Let mixture sit, covered and refrigerated, for about an hour to let flavors blend.
2. Spoon mixture into dumpling wrappers and pinch closed.
3. Cook dumplings.
    a. To fry dumplings, preheat oil in a wok for 30 seconds on high heat, then lower heat to medium. Cook dumplings on each side for about 3 minutes or until golden brown.
    b. To steam dumplings, place in a steamer basket or on an elevated plate in a wok over water on high heat for about 10 minutes.
    c. To boil dumplings, place in boiling water for about 10 minutes.
4. Always cut a dumpling open to make sure it is cooked through.
5. Serve hot with favorite sauce for dipping.

Crazy Dumplings

Pecan Chicken Dumplings

I adore pecans. Growing up we had three huge pecan trees in our backyard and every year we collected bags of pecans for my grandmother to cook with.

- 1 Tbsp oil
- ½ cup chicken, chopped
- Juice of 1 lemon
- 2 garlic cloves, pressed
- ¼ tsp dried basil
- ¼ cup pecans, chopped
- ¼ cup onion, chopped
- ¼ cup broccoli florets, chopped
- ¼ cup cream cheese
- 12 dumpling wrappers
- 1 cup of oil, if frying

1. In a wok, heat oil. Add chicken, lemon juice, garlic, basil, pecans, onion, and broccoli. Sauté until chicken is cooked and onion and broccoli are tender. Remove from heat and then blend with cream cheese.
2. Spoon mixture into dumpling wrappers and pinch closed.
3. To fry dumplings, preheat oil in a wok for 30 seconds on high heat, then lower heat to medium. Cook dumplings on each side for about 3 minutes or until golden brown.
4. Serve hot.

Amanda Roberts

Philly Cheese Steak Pho Dumplings

This dumpling puts an Asian twist on an American favorite.

- ½ cup Nuoc Cham (Spicy Fish Sauce, recipe in the Sauces section)
- 1 Tbsp sugar
- 2 Tbsp cilantro, chopped
- 3 fresh basil leaves, chopped
- 1 small red chili, chopped
- Juice of 1 lime
- 1 cup beef sirloin, chopped
- 1 Tbsp soy sauce
- 1 tsp cayenne pepper
- 2 Tbsp Shaoxing wine
- 1 green onion, chopped
- ¼ cup mozzarella, shredded
- 12 dumpling wrappers
- 1 cup of oil, if frying

1. Whisk together Nuoc Cham, sugar, cilantro, basil, chili, and lime juice in a small bowl until the sugar is dissolved. Set aside.
2. In a bowl, combine beef, soy sauce, pepper, wine, green

onions, and mozzarella.

3. Spoon beef mixture into dumpling wrappers and pinch closed.
4. To fry dumplings, preheat oil in a wok for 30 seconds on high heat, then lower heat to medium. Cook dumplings on each side for about 3 minutes or until golden brown.
5. Always cut a dumpling open to make sure it is cooked through.
6. Serve hot with Nuoc Cham sauce for dipping.

Amanda Roberts

Porcupine Meatball Dumplings

When I told Kickstarter backers that they could suggest a dumpling recipe, I expected to get some Crazy responses. The funny thing is, when Montage Hix suggested a porcupine meatball dumpling, I didn't find the suggestion odd, I was just worried that the average person would not be able to get porcupine meat! Thankfully, the "porcupine meat" in porcupine meatballs is pretty easy to find.

- 1 Tbsp oil
- ¼ cup onion, chopped
- 1 tsp salt
- ½ tsp celery salt
- ½ tsp pepper
- ½ tsp garlic powder
- 1 cup ground meat
- ¼ cup cooked white rice
- 12 dumpling wrappers
- 1 cup of oil, if frying
- Porcupine Sauce for dipping (recipe in the Sauces section)

1. In a wok, heat oil. Add onion, salt, celery, pepper, and garlic powder. Sauté until onion is soft.
2. Add ground meat and cook thoroughly.
3. Add rice and blend. Remove mixture from heat and let cool.
4. Spoon mixture into dumpling wrappers and pinch closed.

Crazy Dumplings

5. To fry dumplings, preheat oil in a wok for 30 seconds on high heat, then lower heat to medium. Cook dumplings on each side for about 3 minutes or until golden brown.
6. Serve hot with Porcupine Sauce for dipping.

Amanda Roberts

Pork with Mango Salsa Dumplings

Pork is a light meat that pairs very well with fruit. This colorful dumpling is perfect for summertime.

- 1 Tbsp oil
- 1 cup ground pork
- Dash of salt
- 1 garlic clove, pressed
- 1 Tbsp chipotle sauce
- ½ cup mango, chopped
- ¼ cup red onion, chopped
- 1 jalapeno, chopped (seeds and ribs removed for less heat)
- Juice of 1 lime
- ¼ cup cilantro, chopped
- 1 Tbsp olive oil
- 1 Tbsp balsamic vinegar
- 12 dumpling wrappers
- 1 cup of oil, if frying

1. In a wok, heat oil. Add pork, salt, garlic, and chipotle sauce. Brown meat. Remove from heat.
2. In a bowl, mix together mango, onion, jalapeno, lime juice, cilantro, olive oil, and vinegar.

Crazy Dumplings

3. Mix meat and ¼ cup of mango salsa together.
4. Spoon mixture into dumpling wrappers and pinch closed.
5. Cook dumplings.
   a. To fry dumplings, preheat oil in a wok for 30 seconds on high heat, then lower heat to medium. Cook dumplings on each side for about 3 minutes or until golden brown.
   b. To steam dumplings, place in a steamer basket or on an elevated plate in a wok over water **on high heat** for about 10 minutes.
   c. To boil dumplings, place in boiling water for about 10 minutes.
6. Serve hot with remaining Mango Salsa for dipping.

Amanda Roberts

Pumpkin and Potato Dumplings

Pumpkin and Potato patties are a popular dish in Malaysia. Here, the patties are bound together inside a dumpling wrapper and served with a spicy dipping sauce. The potato and pumpkin should be steamed soft enough to mash, but not boiled until they are mush.

- ½ cup steamed potato
- ½ cup steamed pumpkin
- 1 tsp fennel
- 1 tsp thyme
- 1 tsp cumin powder
- 1 tsp paprika
- 1 tsp salt
- 1 tsp black pepper
- 1 garlic clove, pressed
- 1 green onion, chopped
- 12 dumpling wrappers
- 1 cup of oil
- Chinese Chili Sauce (recipe in the Sauces section)

Crazy Dumplings

1. In a bowl, mash the potato and pumpkin together.
2. Mix potato mash with all other dumpling ingredients.
3. Spoon mixture into dumpling wrappers and pinch closed.
4. To fry dumplings, preheat oil in a wok for 30 seconds on high heat, then lower heat to medium. Cook dumplings on each side for about 3 minutes or until golden brown.
5. Always cut a dumpling open to make sure it is cooked through.
6. Serve with Chinese Chili Sauce for dipping.

Amanda Roberts

Red Cooked Chicken Dumplings

Red cooked chicken is a very popular dish in Hunan province, where I lived for three years. Even though it isn't typically served in a dumpling, this fun new way to try red cooked chicken is sure to please.

- 1 Tbsp oil
- ½ cup Shaoxing wine
- ¼ cup soy sauce
- ¼ cup brown sugar, packed
- 1 Tbsp Chinese Five Spice Powder
- 1 garlic clove, pressed
- ½ cup chicken, chopped
- ¼ cup carrots, chopped
- ¼ cup broccoli florets, chopped
- ¼ cup snow pea pods, chopped
- 1 green onion, chopped
- 12 dumpling wrappers
- 1 cup of oil

1. In a wok, whisk together oil, wine, soy sauce, brown sugar, Chinese five spice powder, and garlic.
2. Heat sauce and add chicken and veggies. Sauté until chicken is cooked and veggies are tender. Remove from heat and toss with green onions. Let cool enough to handle.

Crazy Dumplings

3. Spoon mixture into dumpling wrappers and pinch closed.
4. To fry dumplings, preheat oil in a wok for 30 seconds on high heat, then lower heat to medium. Cook dumplings on each side for about 3 minutes or until golden brown.
5. Serve hot.

Amanda Roberts

Reindeer Mushroom Dumplings

I just love the interesting recipes that my supporters come up with. Kickstarter backer Jakob requested a reindeer recipe since he lives in Sweden. After a little research, I discovered that reindeer meat is readily available online, but in America we call it caribou meat. I think Americans are just too sentimental to eat Rudolf. You can also substitute the reindeer meat with regular deer meat.

- 1 Tbsp oil
- ¼ cup mushrooms, chopped
- ¼ cup celery, chopped
- ¼ cup onion, chopped
- ½ cup reindeer meat, chopped
- dash of salt
- Dash of pepper
- 12 dumpling wrappers
- 1 cup of oil
- Lingonberry Sauce (recipe in the Sauces section)

1. In a wok, heat oil. Add mushrooms, celery, and onion and sauté until tender.
2. Add reindeer meat, salt, and pepper to wok and stir-fry until meat is cooked through. Remove mixture from heat and let cool enough to handle.

Crazy Dumplings

3. Spoon mixture into dumpling wrappers and pinch closed.
4. To fry dumplings, preheat oil in a wok for 30 seconds on high heat, then lower heat to medium. Cook dumplings on each side for about 3 minutes or until golden brown.
5. Serve hot with Lingonberry Sauce for dipping.

Amanda Roberts

Sausage, Spinach, and Ricotta Dumplings

This Italian-inspired dumpling is best served with a tomato-based sauce, such as the Porcupine Dipping Sauce found in the Sauces section of this book.

- 1 Tbsp oil
- ½ cup Italian sausage
- ½ cup fresh spinach leaves
- ¼ cup water
- ¼ cup ricotta cheese
- ¼ cup mozzarella cheese, shredded
- 1 Tbsp Italian seasoning
- 1 Tbsp garlic powder
- 1 tsp red pepper
- 12 dumpling wrappers
- 1 cup of oil
- Porcupine Dipping Sauce (recipe in the Sauces section)

1. In a wok, heat oil. Add Italian sausage and cook through. Remove from wok and set aside.
2. In the wok, add water and spinach. Sauté until spinach is wilted. Drain. Add sausage to spinach.
3. Add cheeses and seasonings to spinach and sausage. Blend well.

Crazy Dumplings

4. Spoon mixture into dumpling wrappers and pinch closed.
5. Cook dumplings.
    a. To fry dumplings, preheat oil in a wok for 30 seconds on high heat, then lower heat to medium. Cook dumplings on each side for about 3 minutes or until golden brown.
    b. To steam dumplings, place in a steamer basket or on an elevated plate in a wok over water on high heat for about 10 minutes.
    c. To boil dumplings, place in boiling water for about 10 minutes.
6. Always cut a dumpling open to make sure it is cooked through.
7. Serve hot with Porcupine Dipping Sauce.

Amanda Roberts

🦀 Savory Crab Dumplings 🦀

This yummy crab filling is very easy to make whether you use canned or fresh crabmeat. Imitation krab meat might not work as well because it is a bit too sweet. This pairs well with a creamy dipping sauce such as the Alfredo Dipping Sauce found in the Sauces section.

- 1 Tbsp oil
- ¼ cup red bell pepper, chopped
- ¼ cup onion, chopped
- 1 garlic clove, pressed
- ½ cup crabmeat
- Juice and zest of 1 lemon
- 2 tsp capers, drained
- 1 tsp fennel seeds, crushed
- Dash of pepper
- 12 dumpling wrappers
- 1 cup of oil
- Alfredo Dipping Sauce (recipe in the Sauces section)

1. In a wok, heat oil. Add red pepper, onion, and garlic. Sauté until tender.

Crazy Dumplings

2. Add remaining filling ingredients and stir-fry until cooked through. Remove mixture from heat and let cool enough to handle.
3. Spoon mixture into dumpling wrappers and pinch closed.
4. Cook dumplings.
   a. To fry dumplings, preheat oil in a wok for 30 seconds on high heat, then lower heat to medium. Cook dumplings on each side for about 3 minutes or until golden brown.
   b. To steam dumplings, place in a steamer basket or on an elevated plate in a wok over water **on high heat** for about 10 minutes.
   c. To boil dumplings, place in boiling water for about 10 minutes.
5. Serve hot with Alfredo Dipping Sauce.

Amanda Roberts

Sesame Chicken Dumplings

American Chinese food makes great dumpling fillings. In the first Crazy Dumplings Cookbook, I included Orange Chicken Dumplings and Sweet and Sour Chicken Dumplings. For this book, Kickstarter backer Aimee Smith requested Sesame Chicken in a dumpling wrapper. Don't miss General Tsao's Dumplings, also in this book.

- 1 cup chicken, chopped
- 1 cup chicken broth
- 3 Tbsp toasted sesame oil
- 2 Tbsp soy sauce
- 2 Tbsp sugar
- 1 garlic clove, minced
- 1 tsp ginger, microplaned
- 1 tsp chili paste
- 2 Tbsp cornstarch whisked with 2 Tbsp Shaoxing wine
- 12 dumpling wrappers
- 1 cup of oil
- 1 Tbsp toasted sesame seeds
- 1 Tbsp green onions, chopped

1. In a wok, add chicken, chicken broth, sesame oil, sugar, garlic, ginger, and chili paste. Sauté until chicken is cooked through.

Crazy Dumplings

2. Add cornstarch slurry, stirring constantly to thicken the sesame sauce.
3. Once sauce is thick, remove from heat and strain chicken from the sauce. Reserve sauce and let chicken cool.
4. Once the chicken is cool enough to handle, spoon mixture into dumpling wrappers and pinch closed.
5. To fry dumplings, preheat oil in a wok for 30 seconds on high heat, then lower heat to medium. Cook dumplings on each side for about 3 minutes or until golden brown.
6. Always cut a dumpling open to make sure it is cooked through.
7. Plate the dumplings and pour the sesame sauce over them. Sprinkle with the sesame seeds and green onions. Serve hot.

Seitan Fajita Dumplings

Kickstarter backer Delaney Anderson requested a dumpling recipe with seitan. Seitan is a wheat-based meat replacement. Similar to tofu, seitan can be used in the place of almost any meat. Just to demonstrate, here is an updated recipe from the first Crazy Dumplings Cookbook that uses seitan instead of chicken.

- 1 Tbsp oil
- 1 cup seitan, chopped
- ¼ cup bell pepper, chopped
- ¼ cup onion, chopped
- 2 tsp chili powder
- 1 tsp salt
- 1 tsp paprika
- ½ tsp garlic powder
- ¼ tsp cayenne pepper
- ½ tsp cumin
- ¼ cup cheese, shredded
- 12 dumpling wrappers
- 1 cup oil for frying
- Salsa, Guacamole, cheese sauce, sour cream (all possible optional dips; see recipes in the Sauces section)

Crazy Dumplings

1. In a wok, heat oil. Add seitan, bell pepper, onion, and all seasonings together. Sauté until everything is cooked through. Remove from heat and let cool. Blend with shredded cheese.
2. Spoon mixture into dumpling wrappers and pinch closed.
3. To fry dumplings, preheat oil for 30 seconds on high heat, then lower heat to medium. Cook dumplings on each side for about 3 minutes or until golden brown.
4. Serve hot with sauces for dipping.

Amanda Roberts

Spiced Pork Dumplings

This dumpling has a nice wintery flavor to it. It would be delicious served with stuffing and cranberry sauce!

- 1 cup ground pork
- 2 dried bay leaves, ground
- 1 tsp cloves, ground
- ½ tsp black pepper
- 1 tsp sage powder
- 1 tsp sugar
- Dash of salt
- 12 dumpling wrappers
- 1 cup of oil

1. Mix meat and spices together.
2. Spoon mixture into dumpling wrappers and pinch closed.
3. To fry dumplings, preheat oil in a wok for 30 seconds on high heat, then lower heat to medium. Cook dumplings on each side for about 3 minutes or until golden brown.
4. Always cut a dumpling open to make sure it is cooked through.

5. Serve hot with a sweet sauce such as cranberry sauce for dipping.

Spicy Peanut Shrimp Dumplings

This is a Vietnamese inspired dumpling that is sweet and spicy. You can adjust the heat level by removing the seeds and ribs from the chili before mincing.

- 1 tsp ginger, microplaned
- 1 garlic clove, pressed
- Juice of 1 lime
- 1 red chili, chopped
- 1 green onion, chopped
- ¼ cup of cilantro, chopped
- ¼ cup crunchy peanut butter
- ¼ cup fresh mango, chopped
- ½ cup shrimp, peeled, deveined, chopped
- 12 dumpling wrappers
- 1 cup of oil, if frying
- Wasabi Mayo for dipping (recipe in the Sauces section)

1. In a bowl, mix all ingredients together except shrimp. The mixture should have a salad dressing type texture. If it is too thick, add more lime juice.
2. Blend dressing with shrimp.
3. Spoon mixture into dumpling wrappers and pinch closed.

Crazy Dumplings

1. Cook dumplings.

    a. To fry dumplings, preheat oil in a wok for 30 seconds on high heat, then lower heat to medium. Cook dumplings on each side for about 3 minutes or until golden brown.

    b. To steam dumplings, place in a steamer basket or on an elevated plate in a wok over water on high heat for about 10 minutes.

2. Serve hot with Wasabi Mayo for dipping.

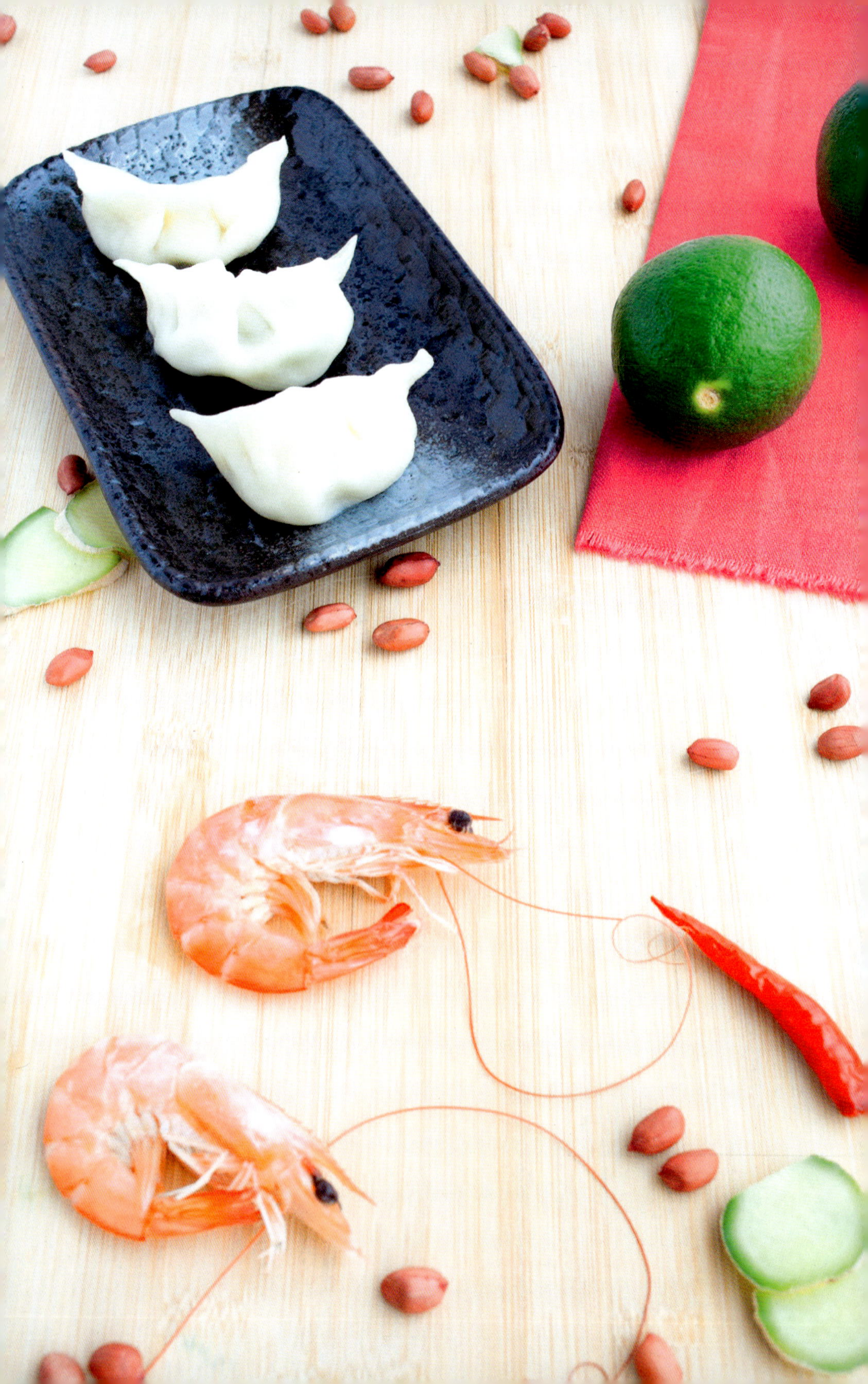

Crazy Dumplings

Spicy Ramen Egg Dumplings

Kickstarter supporter Michelle Huggins requested a dumpling that used egg, ramen, and Sriracha. The result? A dorm room favorite with a twist and kick!

- 1 package of plain ramen noodles
- 1 Tbsp sesame oil
- 2 Tbsp Sriracha sauce
- ¼ cup onion, chopped
- ¼ cup tomato, chopped
- 1 tsp fresh ginger, microplaned
- 1 clove garlic, pressed
- 1 Tbsp soy sauce
- 1 tsp rice vinegar
- 1 green onion, chopped
- 2 Tbsp cilantro, chopped
- 1 egg
- 12 dumpling wrappers
- 1 cup of oil

1. Prepare ramen according to package directions (no need to use seasoning packet). Drain ramen and let cool. Chop ramen and measure out 1 cup of cooked, chopped ramen for use in recipe and set aside. Discard or eat remaining ramen.

2. Mix sesame oil and Siracha together in a wok and bring to a simmer over medium heat. Add onion, tomato, ginger, and garlic and stir-fry until fragrant. Add soy sauce and rice vinegar and bring back to a simmer.
3. Add egg and scramble.
4. Add chopped ramen and blend thoroughly. Remove from heat and let cool.
5. Once mixture is cool enough to handle, spoon mixture into dumpling wrappers and pinch closed.
6. To fry dumplings, preheat oil in a wok for 30 seconds on high heat, then lower heat to medium. Cook dumplings on each side for about 3 minutes or until golden brown.
7. Serve hot with extra Sriracha for dipping.

Spicy Shrimp with Avocado Lime Sauce Dumplings

- 2 Tbsp oil
- 1 cup shrimp, peeled, deveined, chopped
- ¼ cup cherry tomatoes, chopped
- ¼ cup cucumber, chopped
- 1 Tbsp chipotle seasoning
- 1 tsp smoked paprika
- Juice of 1 lime
- Dash of salt
- 1 Tbsp cilantro, chopped
- ¼ cup Avocado Lime Sauce (recipe in the Sauces section)
- 12 dumpling wrappers
- 1 cup of oil, if frying
- Extra Avocado Lime Sauce for dipping

1. In a wok, heat oil. Add shrimp, tomatoes, cucumber, chipotle seasoning, paprika, lime juice, and salt. Sauté until shrimp is cooked and veggies are tender. Remove from heat and let cool enough to handle.
2. Toss shrimp with ¼ cup Avocado Lime Sauce.
3. Spoon mixture into dumpling wrappers and pinch closed.
4. To fry dumplings, preheat oil in a wok for 30 seconds on high

heat, then lower heat to medium. Cook dumplings on each side for about 3 minutes or until golden brown.

5. Always cut a dumpling open to make sure it is cooked through.
6. Serve hot with extra Avocado Lime Sauce for dipping.

Crazy Dumplings

Sriracha Lime Chicken Dumplings

Sriracha seems to be everywhere nowadays, but this dumpling is no fad. You can always substitute the Sriracha with your favorite hot sauce.

- 1 Tbsp Sriracha
- Dash of salt
- Dash of pepper
- 1 Tbsp oil
- Juice and zest of 1 lime
- 1 cup chicken, chopped
- ¼ cup onion, chopped
- 2 Tbsp cilantro, chopped
- 12 dumpling wrappers
- 1 cup of oil
- Avocado Lime Sauce for dipping (recipe in the Sauces section)

1. In a wok, whisk together Sriracha, salt, pepper, oil, and juice. Heat sauce and add chicken and onions. Sauté until chicken is cooked and onion is tender. Remove from heat and let cool. Toss with cilantro and lime zest.
2. Spoon mixture into dumpling wrappers and pinch closed.

3. To fry dumplings, preheat oil in a wok for 30 seconds on high heat, then lower heat to medium. Cook dumplings on each side for about 3 minutes or until golden brown.
4. Always cut a dumpling open to make sure it is cooked through.
5. Serve hot with Avocado Lime Sauce for dipping.

Crazy Dumplings

Sweet and Tangy Tuna Dumplings

This delicious slightly sweet dumpling pairs perfectly with the wasabi mayo found in the Sauces section.

- 1 cup cooked tuna, chopped
- 1 Tbsp soy sauce
- 1 Tbsp teriyaki sauce
- 1 tsp garlic
- 1 Tbsp honey
- 1 tsp ginger, microplaned
- 12 dumpling wrappers
- 1 cup of oil, if frying
- Wasabi Mayo for dipping

1. Mix soy sauce, teriyaki sauce, garlic, honey, and ginger together in a bowl. Blend with tuna and let sit in the refrigerator for an hour for the flavors to mellow.
2. Spoon mixture into dumpling wrappers and pinch closed.
3. Cook dumplings.
    a. To fry dumplings, preheat oil in a wok for 30 seconds on high heat, then lower heat to medium. Cook dumplings on each side for about 3 minutes or until golden brown.
    b. To steam dumplings, place in a steamer basket or on an elevated plate in a wok over water on high heat for about 10 minutes.

4. Always cut a dumpling open to make sure it is cooked through.

Tandoori Chicken Dumplings

An Indian favorite stuffed into a dumpling wrapper.

- 1 Tbsp chili powder
- 1 Tbsp red curry powder
- 1 Tbsp ground cumin
- 1 tsp turmeric
- 1 Tbsp fresh ginger, microplaned
- 5 garlic cloves, pressed
- ¼ cup yogurt
- Juice and zest of 1 lime
- ¼ cup vegetable oil
- Dash of salt
- 1 cup chicken, chopped
- 12 dumpling wrappers
- 1 cup of oil

1. In a bowl, whisk together chili powder, curry, cumin, turmeric, ginger, garlic, yogurt, lime juice and zest, oil, and salt. Add chicken.
2. Heat wok. Add chicken mixture and sauté until chicken is cooked. Remove from heat and drain chicken from sauce. Reserve the sauce and let the chicken cool enough to handle.

3. Spoon mixture into dumpling wrappers and pinch closed.
4. To fry dumplings, preheat oil in a wok for 30 seconds on high heat, then lower heat to medium. Cook dumplings on each side for about 3 minutes or until golden brown.
5. Always cut a dumpling open to make sure it is cooked through.
6. Serve hot with reserved tandoori sauce for dipping.

Crazy Dumplings

Thai Chicken Dumplings

This peanutty dumpling was inspired by delicious Thai food.

- 2 Tbsp peanut butter
- 2 Tbsp soy sauce
- 1 tsp brown sugar
- 1 Tbsp cornstarch whisked with 1 Tbsp water
- 1 Tbsp chicken bullion
- ¼ tsp cayenne pepper
- Dash of salt
- 2 Tbsp oil
- ¼ cup chicken, chopped
- ¼ cup carrots, chopped
- ¼ cup broccoli florets, chopped
- ¼ cup snow pea pods, chopped
- 2 Tbsp peanuts, chopped
- 1 green onion, chopped
- 12 dumpling wrappers
- 1 cup of oil

1. In a bowl, whisk together peanut butter, soy sauce, brown sugar, cornstarch slurry, chicken bouillon, cayenne pepper, and salt. Set aside.
2. In a wok, heat oil and add chicken, carrots, broccoli, and snow pea pods. Sauté until chicken is cooked and veggies are tender. Toss with peanut butter sauce.
3. Remove dumpling filling from heat and let cool enough to handle. Toss with chopped peanuts and green onions.
4. Spoon mixture into dumpling wrappers and pinch closed.
5. To fry dumplings, preheat oil in a wok for 30 seconds on high heat, then lower heat to medium. Cook dumplings on each side for about 3 minutes or until golden brown.
6. Serve hot.

Crazy Dumplings

Tofu, Veggie, and Peanut Dumplings

This is basically a vegetarian version of the Thai Chicken Dumplings, so it is delicious enough for the meat-eaters in your life as well.

- ¼ cup peanut butter
- 1 Tbsp water
- 1 Tbsp vinegar
- 1 Tbsp soy sauce
- 1 Tbsp molasses
- Dash cayenne pepper
- 1 Tbsp oil
- ¼ cup broccoli florets, chopped
- ¼ cup red bell pepper, chopped
- ¼ cup mushrooms, chopped
- ½ cup firm tofu, chopped
- 12 dumpling wrappers
- 1 cup of oil, if frying

1. In a bowl, whisk together peanut butter, water, vinegar, soy sauce, molasses, and cayenne pepper. Set aside.
2. In a wok, heat oil. Add broccoli, bell pepper, mushrooms, and tofu. Sauté until veggies are tender. Toss with peanut butter

sauce. Remove from heat and let cool enough to handle. Drain extra sauce from veggies and reserve.
3. Spoon mixture into dumpling wrappers and pinch closed.
4. To fry dumplings, preheat oil in a wok for 30 seconds on high heat, then lower heat to medium. Cook dumplings on each side for about 3 minutes or until golden brown.
5. Serve hot with reserved sauce for dipping.

Crazy Dumplings

Turkey Bacon Stuffed Dumplings

Of course, you can use any bacon to make this dumpling, but by using turkey bacon, you can pretend it is healthy.

- 4 slices turkey bacon
- ½ cup cream cheese
- 2 green onions, chopped
- 1 clove garlic, pressed
- 12 dumpling wrappers
- 1 cup of oil, if frying

1. Fry bacon until desired crispiness. Remove from heat and chop.
2. In a bowl, combine bacon, cream cheese, green onions, and garlic.
3. Spoon mixture into dumpling wrappers and pinch closed.
4. To fry dumplings, preheat oil in a wok for 30 seconds on high heat, then lower heat to medium. Cook dumplings on each side for about 3 minutes or until golden brown.
5. Serve hot.

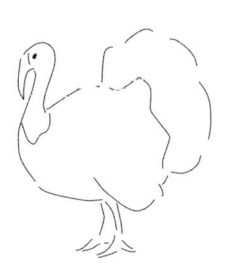

Amanda Roberts

Uzbek Manti

Manti are a dumpling-like food popular throughout Central Asia, including Uzbekistan. Manti are usually served with a cool yogurt for dipping.

- 1 Tbsp oil
- 2 garlic cloves, pressed
- ¼ cup onion, chopped
- 1 tsp toasted cumin
- 1 bay leaf
- 1 Tbsp sesame seeds
- 1 cup ground lamb
- 1 tsp lemon zest
- 1 Tbsp raisins
- 1 Tbsp almonds, crushed
- T Tbsp cilantro, chopped
- 1 Tbsp parsley, chopped
- 1 Tbsp mint, chopped
- 12 dumpling wrappers
- 1 cup of oil, if frying

1. Heat 1 Tbsp oil and add garlic and onion. Sauté until fragrant. Add cumin, bay leaves, and sesame seeds.
2. Add lamb and brown.

Crazy Dumplings

3. Add cilantro, parsley, mint, lemon zest, and raisins. Then add almonds.
4. Remove mixture from heat and let cool enough to handle.
5. Spoon mixture into dumpling wrappers and pinch closed.
   a. To fry dumplings, preheat oil in a wok for 30 seconds on high heat, then lower heat to medium. Cook dumplings on each side for about 3 minutes or until golden brown.
   b. To steam dumplings, place in a steamer basket or on an elevated plate in a wok over water **on high heat** for about 10 minutes.
   c. To boil dumplings, place in boiling water for about 10 minutes.
6. Serve hot with yogurt for dipping.

Amanda Roberts

Vietnamese Meatball Mango Dumplings

I recently went to Vietnam mainly because of the food. The most important question to ask before visiting any country is "what's the food like?" While these dumplings are amazing on their own, when paired with the Green Cashew Sauce in the Sauces section, they take you to a new plain of deliciousness. This one is a must try!

- 1 Tbsp sesame oil
- ½ cup ground pork sausage
- 1 Tbsp soy sauce
- 1 Tbsp Nuoc Cham (Spicy Fish Sauce, recipe in the Sauces section)
- 1 Tbsp honey
- ¼ cup mango, chopped
- ¼ cup carrot, chopped
- ¼ cup cucumber, chopped
- ¼ cup red onion, chopped
- 1 chili pepper, chopped
- Juice of 1 lime
- 12 dumpling wrappers
- 1 cup of oil, if frying
- Green Cashew Sauce for dipping (recipe in the Sauces section)

Crazy Dumplings

1. In a wok, heat 1 Tbsp sesame oil. Add sausage, soy sauce, Nuoc Cham, and honey. Cook sausage through. Remove from heat.
2. Toss pork with remaining filling ingredients.
3. Spoon mixture into dumpling wrappers and pinch closed.
4. To fry dumplings, preheat oil in a wok for 30 seconds on high heat, then lower heat to medium. Cook dumplings on each side for about 3 minutes or until golden brown.
5. Serve hot with Green Cashew Sauce for dipping.

Amanda Roberts

Sweet Dumplings

Crazy Dumplings

Banana Cream Dumplings

This dumpling is kind of like a fried banana cream pie. Warm, creamy, and delicious!

- ½ cup cream cheese
- ¼ cup sugar
- ¼ cup sour cream
- 2 Tbsp banana liquor
- 1 tsp vanilla extract
- 1 ripe banana
- 12 dumpling wrappers
- 1 cup of oil
- Whipped cream for topping

1. In a bowl, mix cream cheese and sugar. Stir in sour cream, banana liquor, and vanilla. Mash in banana. Stir until mixture is smooth.
2. Spoon mixture into dumpling wrappers.
3. To fry dumplings, preheat oil in a wok for 30 seconds on high heat, then lower heat to medium. Cook dumplings on each side for about 3 minutes or until golden brown.
4. Serve hot with a dollop (or mountain) of whipped cream on each one.

Amanda Roberts

Blackberry Dumplings

When I was a kid, we had blackberry bushes as large as trees in our backyard, and it was always a treat when they ripened in the summer. Here in China, farmers sell blackberries out of baskets on every street when they come into season. Enjoy a taste of summer with these messy and yummy dumplings.

- 1 cup blackberries
- Juice of 1 lemon
- ¼ cup sugar
- 1 Tbsp cornstarch
- ½ cup powdered sugar
- 1 Tbsp milk (more or less to adjust constancy)
- 12 dumpling wrappers
- 1 cup of oil

1. In a bowl, toss blackberries, juice, sugar, and cornstarch together. Let set for 20 minutes, tossing and coarsely mashing occasionally.
2. Spoon mixture into dumpling wrappers.
3. To fry dumplings, preheat oil in a wok for 30 seconds on high heat, then lower heat to medium. Cook dumplings on each side for about 3 minutes or until golden brown.

Crazy Dumplings

4. In another bowl, whisk together powdered sugar and milk to make icing.
5. Drizzle icing over dumplings and serve.

Amanda Roberts

Blueberry Cream Dumplings

This dumpling is also a fun summer treat.

- ¼ cup sugar
- 1 Tbsp cinnamon
- ¼ cup marshmallow cream
- ¼ cup whipped cream cheese
- ½ cup blueberries
- 12 dumpling wrappers
- 1 cup of oil

1. In a bowl, whisk together sugar and cinnamon. Set aside.
2. In a blender, add marshmallow cream, cream cheese, and blueberries. Mix on low speed until thoroughly blended.
3. Spoon blueberry mixture into dumpling wrappers.
4. To fry dumplings, preheat oil in a wok for 30 seconds on high heat, then lower heat to medium. Cook dumplings on each side for about 3 minutes or until golden brown.
5. Lightly dab each dumpling into the sugar mixture until evenly coated and serve.

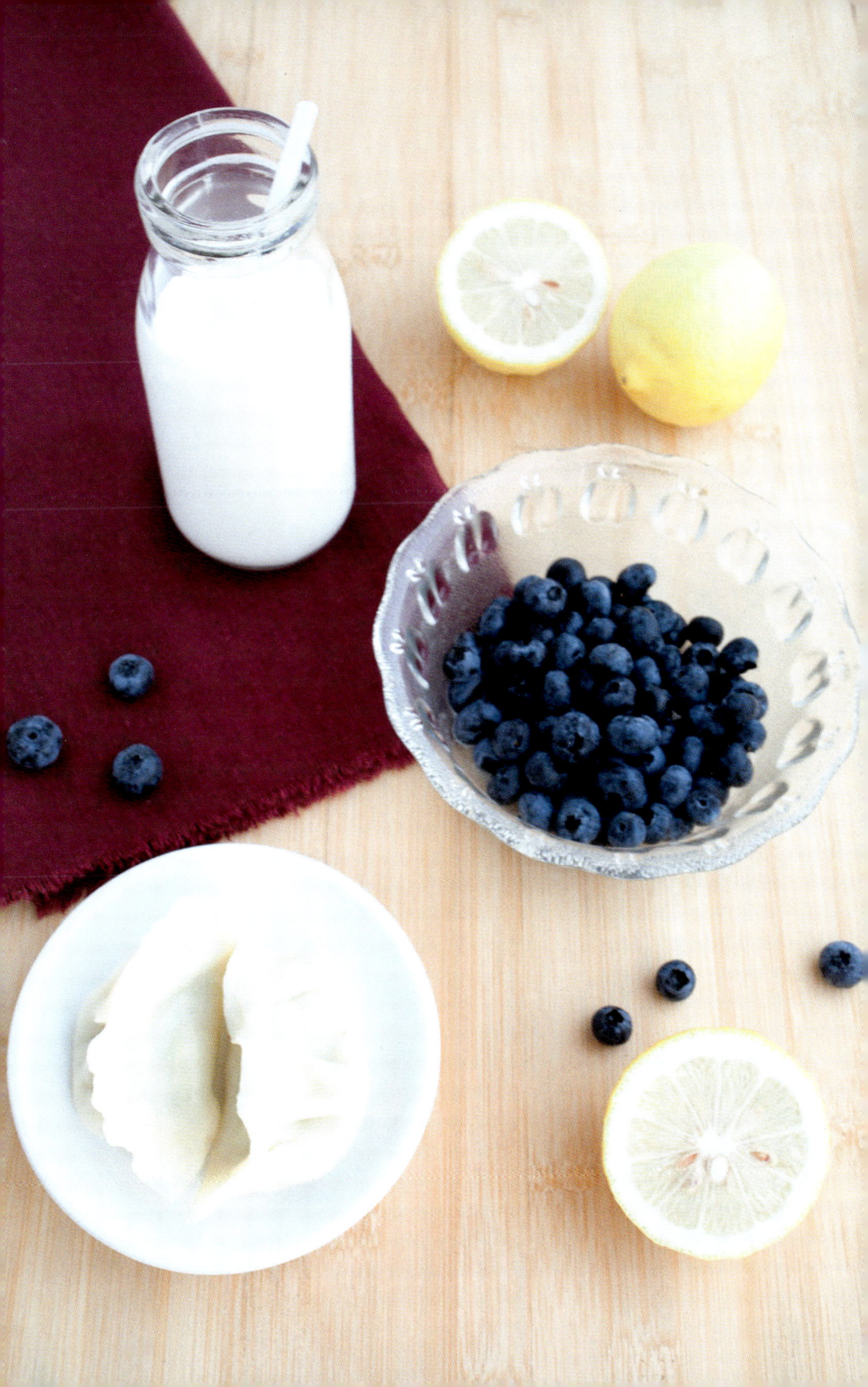

Amanda Roberts

Chocolate Covered Cherry Dumplings

Kickstarter backer Louise Williams requested a cherry marzipan recipe, which already sounded delicious, but I took it a step further by adding ingredients typically found in chocolate covered cherries. These are simply divine!

- 12 cherries, pitted and quartered
- 2 Tbsp rum or brandy
- ½ cup almonds, ground and toasted
- 12 pieces of marzipan
- 1 bar of milk chocolate, 1.5 oz.
- 12 dumpling wrappers
- 1 cup of oil

1. In a bowl, soak the cherries in the liquor for about an hour, then drain the cherries and pat them dry with a paper towel.
2. Place 1 piece of marzipan, 4 cherry quarters, and ½ Tbsp of toasted almonds into each dumpling wrapper and pinch closed.
3. To fry dumplings, preheat oil in a wok for 30 seconds on high heat, then lower heat to medium. Cook dumplings on each side for about 3 minutes or until golden brown.

Crazy Dumplings

4. In a double boiler or a microwave, melt the chocolate bar. Drizzle melted chocolate over dumplings or serve as a dip.

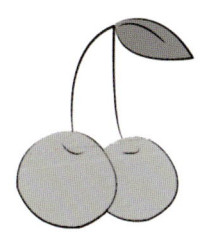

Amanda Roberts

Kaya Dumplings

Kaya is a Malaysian coconut egg jam. What makes kaya so special is pandan leaves. Pandan leaves are easy to find in Asia, but more difficult to find in the West. You can usually find them at Chinese, Vietnamese, or Thai supermarkets. If you can't find fresh pandan leaves, you can also use canned pandan extract. Just be sure you freeze any you don't use after opening as it has a short shelf life.

- 2 eggs
- ¼ cup coconut cream
- ½ cup coconut milk
- 2 pandan leaves, tied into a knot
- 1 Tbsp cornstarch whisked with 1 Tbsp water
- ½ cup sugar whisked with 2 Tbsp water
- 12 dumpling wrappers
- 1 cup of oil

1. In a bowl, whisk the eggs, coconut cream, coconut milk, and sugar.
2. Transfer the egg mixture into a wok. Add the pandan leaves and turn on the heat to medium low. Using a wood spatula or a pair of wooden chopsticks, keep stirring the mixture until they are cooked, about 20 minutes. Whisk in the cornstarch slurry to thicken. Please take note that lumps will form in the jam. Set aside.
3. In a saucepan, heat up the sugar water over medium heat,

swirling gently, until the sugar melts into caramel. When the color becomes golden brown, add the caramel to the kaya. Stir to combine well. The color of the kaya should be golden brown.

4. After the kaya jam cools, discard the pandan leaves. The kaya jam should have a smooth, creamy texture. If it doesn't, you can use a hand mixer.

5. Spoon kaya into dumpling wrappers and pinch closed.

6. To fry dumplings, preheat oil in a wok for 30 seconds on high heat, then lower heat to medium. Cook dumplings on each side for about 3 minutes or until golden brown.

7. Serve hot.

Amanda Roberts

Lemon Meringue Dumplings

Lemon meringue pie in a dumpling.

- 2 eggs
- 2 Tbsp cornstarch
- ¾ cup sugar
- 3 Tbsp sugar
- ¾ cup water
- Juice and zest of 1 lemon
- 1 ½ Tbsp butter
- 12 dumpling wrappers
- 1 cup of oil

1. Separate the egg whites from the egg yolks and set both aside.
2. In a saucepan, whisk together cornstarch, ¾ cup of sugar, and water.
3. Add the lemon juice, zest, and yolks and cook over medium heat, stirring constantly, until the mixture begins to bubble and thicken.
4. Remove from heat and then whisk in butter. Set aside.
5. In a bowl, whip egg whites into soft peaks. Add 3 tablespoons of sugar in a slow, steady stream and continue to beat until the whites have increased to about six times the volume and

are glossy and firm. Set aside.
6. Fill dumpling wrappers with lemon mixture.
7. To fry dumplings, preheat oil in a wok for 30 seconds on high heat, then lower heat to medium. Cook dumplings on each side for about 3 minutes or until golden brown.
8. Serve hot with a dab (or a mountain) of meringue on each one.

Amanda Roberts

Peach Pie Dumplings

Peaches are naturally sweet, so it doesn't take too much sugar to make these delicious dumplings. Serve with ice cream for Peach Pie Dumplings alamode!

- 1 cups peaches, peeled and chopped
- ¼ cup sugar
- ¼ cup water
- 1 cinnamon stick
- 2 cloves
- 12 dumpling wrappers
- 1 cup of oil

1. In a saucepan, combine all filling ingredients. Bring to a boil over medium heat. Cook until peaches are softened. Drain excess water and remove cinnamon stick and cloves.
2. Mash peaches. Cook over low heat for another 15 minutes, stirring constantly to prevent burning. Remove from heat and let cool enough to handle.
3. Spoon peach mixture into dumpling wrappers and pinch closed.
4. To fry dumplings, preheat oil in a wok for 30 seconds on high heat, then lower heat to medium. Cook dumplings on each side for about 3 minutes or until golden brown.
5. Serve hot, sprinkled with cinnamon and sugar and with a scoop of ice cream.

Crazy Dumplings

Peanut Butter Chocolate Dumplings

Because peanut butter and chocolate are the most perfect pairing.

- ½ cup peanut butter (crunchy or creamy)
- ¼ cup sugar
- ¼ cup chocolate chips
- 12 dumpling wrappers
- 1 cup of oil

1. In a bowl, combine peanut butter, sugar, and chocolate chips.
2. Spoon mixture into dumpling wrappers and pinch closed.
3. To fry dumplings, preheat oil in a wok for 30 seconds on high heat, then lower heat to medium. Cook dumplings on each side for about 3 minutes or until golden brown.
4. Serve hot.

Amanda Roberts

Prune Dumplings with Toffee Sauce

Prunes get a bad rap simply because they help keep you regular. They are actually really delicious and are decadent when paired with this toffee sauce.

- 1 cup pitted prunes
- ¼ cup sugar
- 1 Tbsp vanilla and 1 tsp vanilla
- 1 Tbsp cinnamon powder
- 12 dumpling wrappers
- 1 cup of oil
- ¼ cup unsalted butter
- ½ cup packed brown sugar

Juice of 1 lemon

1. In a saucepan, cover prunes with water and boil for 10 minutes. Drain Liquid, reserving ¼ cup.
2. Puree prunes in a blender or with a hand mixer. Add puree back to the saucepan with sugar, vanilla, cinnamon, and reserved liquid.
3. Cook over low heat, stirring regularly until mixture thickens. Remove from heat and let cool enough to handle.
4. Spoon puree into dumpling wrappers and pinch to close.

Crazy Dumplings

5. To fry dumplings, preheat oil in a wok for 30 seconds on high heat, then lower heat to medium. Cook dumplings on each side for about 3 minutes or until golden brown. Set dumpling aside.
6. Melt butter over medium heat and add brown sugar. Once mixture is boiling, add lemon juice and 1 tsp vanilla. Remove from heat.
7. Toss Prune Dumplings with Toffee Sauce and serve.

Amanda Roberts

Pumpkin Cream Cheese Dumplings

This autumn dumpling might replace your pumpkin pie on your holiday table this year.

- ½ cup cream cheese
- ½ cup canned pumpkin filling
- 1 tsp vanilla extract
- 1 Tbsp brown sugar
- 1 ½ Tbsp white sugar
- 1 tsp cinnamon
- 1 Tbsp pecans, chopped
- 12 dumpling wrappers
- 1 cup of oil
- Whipped cream for topping

1. Blend all of the filling ingredients.
2. Spoon pumpkin mixture into dumpling wrappers and pinch closed.
3. To fry dumplings, preheat oil in a wok for 30 seconds on high heat, then lower heat to medium. Cook dumplings on each side for about 3 minutes or until golden brown.

4. Serve hot with a dab (or a mountain) of whipped cream on each one.

Amanda Roberts

🍓 Strawberry Chocolate Dumplings 🍓

These strawberry dumplings that you can dip in brown sugar sauce would make a great Valentine's Day treat for your sweetie!

- 1 cup strawberries, chopped
- Juice of 1 lemon
- ½ cup balsamic vinegar
- ¼ cup and 2 Tbsp. brown sugar
- ½ cup chocolate chips
- 12 dumpling wrappers
- 1 cup of oil
- 2 Tbsp powdered sugar

1. In a bowl, mix strawberries and lemon juice. Let sit for about 20 minutes.
2. In a saucepan, heat vinegar and ¼ cup brown sugar to a simmer. Let simmer until reduced by half.
3. Spoon strawberries and some of the chocolate chips into each dumpling wrapper and pinch closed.
4. To fry dumplings, preheat oil in a wok for 30 seconds on high heat, then lower heat to medium. Cook dumplings on each side for about 3 minutes or until golden brown.
5. Serve hot dusted with powdered sugar and drizzled with brown sugar sauce.

Strawberry Cheesecake Dumplings

I could probably have made the whole Sweet Dumplings section just strawberry-based recipes, but I restrained myself. There are just so many yummy things you can do with strawberries!

- ½ cup cream cheese
- 1 Tbsp sour cream
- ½ cup sugar, divided
- ½ Tbsp vanilla
- ½ cup strawberries, chopped
- 12 dumpling wrappers
- 1 cup of oil
- 1 Tbsp cinnamon

1. In a bowl, mix cream cheese, sour cream, 1 Tbsp sugar, and vanilla. Blend in strawberries.
2. Spoon cheesecake filling into a dumpling wrapper and pinch closed.
3. To fry dumplings, preheat oil in a wok for 30 seconds on high heat, then lower heat to medium. Cook dumplings on each side for about 3 minutes or until golden brown.
4. On a plate, blend remaining sugar and cinnamon. Dip dumplings in sugar mixture to coat and serve.

Amanda Roberts

Sweet Rice and Raisin Dumplings

This sweet rice and raisin dumpling is sometimes used as an empanada filling. Like dumplings, empanada wrappers are great vehicles for a variety of fillings, so empanada recipes are easily adaptable for dumplings.

- ½ cup long-grain white rice
- 1 cup water
- 1 large cinnamon stick
- Dash of salt
- ½ cup evaporated milk
- ¼ cup condensed milk
- ¼ cup raisins
- 1 tsp vanilla extract
- ¼ cup sweetened coconut, shredded (optional)
- Powdered sugar for dusting
- 12 dumpling wrappers
- 1 cup of oil

1. In a large saucepan, add the rice, water, cinnamon stick, and salt. Bring to a boil, lower heat, and cook until most of the water has been absorbed.
2. Stir in milks and continue cooking for approximately 5 more minutes. Add raisins and cook for 2 more minutes.

Crazy Dumplings

3. Remove from heat and let cool.
4. Spoon mixture into dumpling wrappers along with a bit of coconut and pinch closed.
5. To fry dumplings, preheat oil in a wok for 30 seconds on high heat, then lower heat to medium. Cook dumplings on each side for about 3 minutes or until golden brown.
6. Lightly dust with powdered sugar and serve.

Amanda Roberts

🍅 Sweet Tomato Dumplings 🍅

I never would have thought of tomatoes as a sweet dessert until I learned sweet tomato paste is a popular filling for empanadas. It sounded crazy enough to me, so I came up with this dumpling version.

- 6 roma tomatoes
- 1 cinnamon stick
- 3 cloves
- ½ cup brown sugar
- 1 Tbsp cornstarch
- 12 dumpling wrappers
- 1 cup of oil
- 2 Tbsp powdered sugar

1. Peel and deseed the tomatoes. In a non-stick pot, mash the tomatoes. Add the cinnamon and cloves. Over low heat, cook the tomatoes, stirring constantly so they do not burn. Boil for about 45 minutes so the tomatoes release all their water.
2. Strain the water away from the tomato puree, reserving about 2 Tbsp of the liquid. Also remove the cinnamon stick and cloves.
3. In the pot, mix the tomato puree with the brown sugar. Return to a boil and cook for about 30 more minutes. Add

Crazy Dumplings

more sugar if needed.

4. Mix the cornstarch with the reserved tomato water. Add the cornstarch slurry to the tomato puree. Cook for another 15 minutes, until the consistency is like paste, though the mixture will thicken as it cools. Remove from heat and let tomato paste cool enough to handle.
5. Spoon mixture into dumpling wrappers and pinch closed.
6. To fry dumplings, preheat oil in a wok for 30 seconds on high heat, then lower heat to medium. Cook dumplings on each side for about 3 minutes or until golden brown.
7. Serve hot dusted with powdered sugar.

🍍Tropical Fruit Dumplings🍍

This is summer in a dumpling! Try using new fruits you don't normally eat for a unique flavor. You can change the fruits every time you make this so the recipe never gets old.

- 1 cup mixed tropical fruit, chopped (like jackfruit, mango, pineapple, prickly pear, etc.)
- 1 Tbsp fresh mint, chopped
- ¼ cup brown sugar
- 1 tsp Chinese five-spice powder
- 12 dumpling wrappers
- 1 cup of oil

1. In a bowl, mix fruits, mint, sugar, and five-spice powder together.
2. Spoon mixture into dumpling wrappers and pinch closed.
3. To fry dumplings, preheat oil in a wok for 30 seconds on high heat, then lower heat to medium. Cook dumplings on each side for about 3 minutes or until golden brown.
4. Serve hot.

Crazy Dumplings

Sauces

Amanda Roberts

Alfredo Dipping Sauce

This easy Alfredo sauce pairs well with several dumplings in this book, or you can serve it over noodles or rice for a quick meal.

- ¼ cup butter
- 4 ounces cream cheese
- 1 Tbsp garlic powder
- 1 cup milk
- ¼ cup parmesan cheese
- Dash of black pepper

1. Melt butter in a non-stick saucepan over medium heat. Add cream cheese and garlic powder. Use a whisk to blend well.
2. Slowly add the milk, whisking all the time. Add parmesan cheese and pepper.
3. Remove from heat when sauce reaches desired consistency.
4. Best served hot.

Avocado Lime Sauce

While I only pair this with a couple of dumplings in the book, it is insanely delicious and versatile. I would put this on everything, especially anything Mexican. Make a double or triple batch and keep in it the fridge next to your salsa for a delicious dip option.

- 1 avocado
- Juice of 3 limes
- 1 Tbsp olive oil
- 1 tsp garlic powder
- Dash of salt

1. Mash avocado as fine as possible and then whisk all ingredients together until smooth.
2. Chill until ready to serve.

Amanda Roberts

Chinese Chili Sauce

Chinese Chili Sauce is very spicy, so it goes great with mild dumplings, or feel free to pair it with the spicy dumplings in the book if you like to live dangerously.

- 10 dried red chilies
- 1 cup hot water
- 1 garlic clove, pressed
- 2 Tbsp brown sugar
- 1 tsp salt
- 4 Tbsp white vinegar
- 2 Tbsp sesame oil

1. Soak the chilies in hot water for about 20 minutes.
2. Put softened chilies, garlic, sugar, salt, and vinegar into a blender and grind to desired texture. Remove chili paste from blender and set aside.
3. Heat sesame oil in a wok until it starts to smoke. Remove from heat.
4. In a bowl, combine chili paste and sesame oil. Mix well.
5. Let sauce cool completely before transferring to an airtight container and refrigerating.
    - 10 dried red chilies

Crazy Dumplings

- 1 cup hot water
- 1 pressed garlic clove
- 2 Tbsp brown sugar
- 1 tsp salt
- 4 Tbsp white vinegar
- 2 Tbsp sesame oil

6. Soak the chilies in hot water for about 20 minutes.
7. Put softened chilies, garlic, sugar, salt, and vinegar into a blender and grind to desired texture. Remove chili paste from blender and set aside.
8. Heat sesame oil in a wok until it starts to smoke. Remove from heat.
9. In a bowl, combine chili paste and sesame oil. Mix well.
10. Let sauce cool completely before transferring to an airtight container and refrigerating.

Amanda Roberts

Chipotle Mayonnaise

This spicy mayo is great as a dip, but it also works as a sandwich spread. I love it on turkey and tuna fish sandwiches!

- 1 cup mayonnaise
- 1 Tbsp chipotle powder
- 1 tsp garlic powder
- 1 tsp paprika
- Juice of 1 lime
- Dash of salt (or to taste)

1. In a bowl, whisk together all ingredients.
2. Store leftover sauce in an airtight container and refrigerate.

Green Cashew Sauce

This fragrant green sauce is a good one to keep in the fridge because you never know when it will pair well with whatever you are eating.

- ¼ cup fresh cilantro
- ¼ cup fresh basil
- ¾ cups roasted cashews
- ¼ cup milk, plus more if needed
- Juice of 2 limes
- 1 tsp red pepper
- 2 Tbsp Thai Sweet Chili Sauce (recipe in the Sauces section)

1. Combine all ingredients in a blender and blend until smooth. Feel free to taste and adjust ingredients as needed.
2. Store leftover sauce in an airtight container and refrigerate.

Amanda Roberts

Lingonberry Sauce

This sweet sauce perfectly pairs with the Reindeer Dumplings, but I think it would also be wonderful as an ice cream topping!

- 1 ¾ cups beef stock
- 1 ¾ cups sweet cranberry juice
- Juice of 1 lemon
- 2 tsp sugar
- 1 Tbsp cornstarch whisked in 1 Tbsp water
- 2 Tbsp cream
- ¼ cup lingonberries

1. Combine the stock and 1 cup of the cranberry juice in a saucepan and simmer until reduced to about ¼ of a cup. It should be very thick.
2. Add the remaining juice, the lemon juice, and the sugar. Heat back to a simmer and make sure all the sugar is dissolved.
3. Add the cornstarch slurry and cream to sauce. Bring back to a simmer.
4. Add berries and bring back to a simmer.
5. The sauce can be served hot or chilled.
6. Store leftover sauce in an airtight container and refrigerate.

Crazy Dumplings

Honey Chipotle Sauce

Sweet and spicy, this sauce pairs well with dumplings that have a more delicate flavor.

- 4 Tbsp honey
- Juice of 1 lime
- 1 Tbsp chipotle sauce
- 1 Tbsp soy sauce

1. In a bowl, whisk together all ingredients.
2. Store leftover sauce in an airtight container and refrigerate.

Nuoc Cham (Vietnamese Spicy Fish Sauce)

This Spicy Fish Sauce – Nuoc Cham in Vietnamese – goes perfectly with the Vietnamese dumplings in this book. Fish sauce can usually be found in the Asian section of any supermarket.

- 1 garlic clove, pressed
- 1 hot chili pepper, chopped (or more depending on heat level desired)
- ½ Tbsp sugar
- Juice of 1 lime
- ½ cup fish sauce
- 2 ½ Tbsp water

1. In a small bowl, combine garlic, chili pepper, sugar, and lime juice.
2. Add fish sauce and water. Whisk all ingredients together and chill until ready to serve.
3. Store leftover sauce in an airtight container and refrigerate.

Crazy Dumplings

Porcupine Dipping Sauce

This recipe makes a great tomato based dipping sauce. It was designed to go with the Porcupine Meatball Dumplings, but you could pair it with many savory dumplings.

- 1 can (15 ounces) tomato sauce
- 1 cup water
- 2 tablespoons brown sugar
- 2 teaspoons Worcestershire sauce

1. In a saucepan, combine all ingredients. Over low heat, stir constantly until brown sugar dissolves and the mixture is heated through.
2. Serve as a dip alongside dumplings.
3. Store leftover sauce in an airtight container and refrigerate.

Salsa

Of course, it is easy and cheap to buy a jar of salsa in most Western countries, but in China, it is expensive and can be difficult to find. But even if you live in the West, try using this easy recipe for a small amount of homemade salsa! It's always better to cook local and organic when you can, so give it a try. Also, if you just finely chop and mix the ingredients but don't cook them, you'll have a delicious pico de gallo.

- 6 medium-sized tomatoes (~2 pounds worth), peeled, seeds removed, chopped
- 1 onion, chopped
- 1 green bell pepper, chopped
- 1 jalapeno, chopped (seeds and ribs removed for less heat)
- 2 garlic cloves, pressed
- 2 Tbsp fresh cilantro, chopped
- Juice of 1 lemon
- ¼ tsp oregano
- 1 tsp black pepper
- Dash of salt

1. Put all the ingredients in a saucepan and gently bring to a simmer.
2. Taste mixture as it cooks. Add salt to taste.

3. Remove from heat when salsa reaches desired taste/consistency.
4. Let it cool before transferring to an airtight container and refrigerating. Salsa can keep for about 4 weeks.

Amanda Roberts

Thai Sweet Chili Sauce

This sauce goes great with so many dumplings, from Traditional Dumplings to Sweet and Sour Chicken Dumplings. This recipe makes a small amount, but feel free to double or triple it to keep a jar around to use with dumplings and lots of other foods that need a sweet and spicy kick.

- 3 garlic cloves, pressed
- 2 red jalapeno or Serrano peppers (seeds and ribs removed for less heat)
- ¼ cup white distilled vinegar
- ½ cup sugar
- ¾ cup water
- ½ Tbsp salt
- 1 Tbsp cornstarch whisked with 1 Tbsp water

1. Combine all ingredients in a blender except for cornstarch slurry. Puree ingredients.
2. Transfer mixture to a saucepan and bring to a boil over medium heat. Simmer mixture until it begins to thicken.
3. Whisk cornstarch slurry into the chili mixture and simmer sauce for one more minute.
4. Let sauce cool completely before transferring to an airtight container and refrigerating.

Wasabi Mayo

This spicy mayo is a lovely pairing with some of the milder dumplings such as the Sweet and Tangy Tuna.

- ½ cup mayo
- 7 oz. Greek yogurt
- 3 tsp wasabi
- Juice of 1 lime
- Dash of salt

1. Whisk all ingredients together and chill until ready to serve.
2. Store leftover sauce in an airtight container and refrigerate.

Amanda Roberts

Metric Conversions

One of the biggest issues with being an American trying to cook in China is the metric conversions, so I've included this handy chart to help you adapt the recipes to however you are comfortable.

Volume Conversions

U.S. Volume Measure	Metric Equivalent
1/8 teaspoon	0.5 milliliters
¼ teaspoon	1 milliliter
½ teaspoon	2 milliliters
1 teaspoon	5 milliliters
½ tablespoon	7 milliliters
1 tablespoon (3 teaspoons)	15 milliliters
2 tablespoons (1 fluid ounce)	30 milliliters
¼ cup (4 tablespoons)	60 milliliters
1/3 cup	90 milliliters
½ cup (4 fluid ounces)	125 milliliters
2/3 cup	160 milliliters
¾ cup (6 fluid ounces)	180 milliliters
1 cup (16 tablespoons)	250 milliliters
1 pint (2 cups)	500 milliliters
1 quart (4 CUPS)	1 liter

Weight Conversions

U.S. Weight Measure	Metric Equivalent
½ ounce	15 grams
1 ounce	30 grams
2 ounce	60 grams
3 ounce	85 grams
¼ pound (4 ounces)	115 grams
½ pound (8 ounces)	225 grams
¾ pound (12 ounces)	340 grams
1 pound (16 ounces)	454 grams

Oven Temperature Conversions

Degrees Fahrenheit	Degrees Celsius
200 degrees F	95 degrees C
250 degrees F	120 degrees C
275 degrees F	135 degrees C
300 degrees F	150 degrees C
325 degrees F	160 degrees C
350 degrees F	180 degrees C
375 degrees F	190 degrees C
400 degrees F	205 degrees C
425 degrees F	220 degrees C
450 degrees F	230 degrees C

About the Author

Amanda Roberts is an American writer, editor, and teacher who has been living in China since 2010. She has an MA in English and has published books, short stories, articles, poems, and essays in publications all over the world. She blogs about her life in China at *Two Americans in China* and heads the Women Writers of Shenzhen writers circle. She can be found all over the Internet.

http://www.twoamericansinchina.com/

https://www.facebook.com/TwoAmericansinChina

https://twitter.com/2americanschina

http://www.pinterest.com/amandachina/crazy-dumplings/

Email her: twoamericansinchina@gmail.com

Crazy Dumplings

Thank You!

This book would not have been possible without the hundreds of people who supported it on Kickstarter! Thank you to the Craziest backers on the planet!

fgfdg	David Spaxman	Zachary Brumleve
Louise Williams	Chris Edwards (aka 郝丘)	Dan Kinder
Aimee M. Smith	Michael M. Kroeker	Kyle K
Montage Hix	Anthony Ryan Ortiz	Martina Dvořáková
Jakob de Pina Pääjärvi	Candace Fetzer	The Eiche-Huggins Family
Kim Dyer	RCoke	Marijo Yates
Kit Wickliff	Margaret St. John	Kate Scott
Daniel Lanigan	Nicholas Smillie	Eileen Hendriksen
James Yuen	Scott Loonan	Joseph Moyer
HJ	J.	Erik Singer
Stefan Winkler	Krista L. Griffiths	Max Zomborszki
Mark Henderson	Keith Solomon	Lenaldo Rocha
Brandon Inoue	Donna Nutter	Joshua D Olenik
Victor E.	A Jacob Cord	Steffen Heise
Kimberley Timmings	Rob McKeagney	James McKendrew
Neil Graham	Aaron Bretveld	Jennifer M. Brown
Dane & Vera	AC	Jonathon Zachariah
Marina	Dan Canz	Visalachy Sittampalam
Sara Doty	Pip	Josh Garneau
Regan Smith	Heather Whittaker	Damian Morgan
Jessica Welke-Schaeffer	Bruce Martin	Sara H. Lappi
Johan Buts aka YoYo	Eileen LaBoone	Jessica Slavik

Amanda Roberts

Amelia Hite and Fam	Camey Johnson	Schiltz G.
C.Tamura	Jess Dulin	William Hall
Angela Pritchett	Tina Young	Laura Lundy
Daria M.	Ahad M.	Koendert Ruifrok
Keba Jackson	R.S. Dixon	Rob Steinberger
Viv	Dean Gillis	Thilo von Trotha
Shauna M. Ratliff	Andrew Stiemke	EB&Milo
kk	Hilla Heikkilä	Bee Gallagher
Pamela Izzo	Kyle Trudel	Ellen Harwood
tofuji	Carrie Lillie-Lugo	Josh
Aaron Beard	Vidya Gopalakrishna	Kelly DeSando
Anita Briamonte	Megan Hilliard	Dumpling Lover
Dan Watson	Kelly Beecher	Rachael LaMielle
Brandon Marris	Dwight Bishop	Sanchini Family
Arion Hypes	Ruth Tedman Hartstein	Scott Homann
Sarah Do	Angela Chatha	Benushka
Theresa Weidner	Nigel T H Perera in Qatar	Ron Hollatz
Raquel Orozco	Bruce Bellak	Sarah Golon
Dennis Zander	MJ DeHart	Susannah Watt
Katie "Da Best" Forshey	exNaClH2O	Amy "Dumpling Gang" Laurent
Jules cooper	Megan Trahan	Tim and Hannah Meakins
Christian K.	Joshua C. Martin	Jol
Felicia Brown	Gail Lowson	Matt Hardin
Hazel O'Keeffe	Sarah Alhas	Aaron White
Billy Ingle	Alex Black	Bonnie Ward
Ruud van Ierland	stacy blois	Jacob and Mayet
Jason Griffin	Michael Salter	Jason V.
Katy Hill	Steve Eldridge	John Long

Crazy Dumplings

Megz Cantara
Amanda Bell
Jimmy Law
Ian 'Smurf' Murphy
Laura Beasley
Bill Johnson
Panderps
James J Moe
Amy Sept
Justin & Andrea
Alison Radzun
Eric White
Tanya Noreen
Neville Isles
James Hutton
T.Tran
Chicago
Ashley Rommel
Florian Schupp
Gunnar Heide Aadland
Jess Webster
Reece Liddicoat
Scott Bain
Jessica Weinberg
Saruta
Dawn Cullity
Amanda Miller
Joan & Pau

Julie and Ziggy Viens
Fabrice A.
Sarah Reeves
Vonny
Dimitri van Dijk
Samantha Dorr
SB Living
Jay & Grace
Breanna Hodges
Samantha Meyer
Judy A. Ospital
Kate Lindinger
Rob J. D.
Kristie Macris
Daniel Einschlag
Alana Duran
Khrysey C
Dan C
Keith Travis
Theodore Savvas Donta
Sommer Louie
Nissa Cady
Ellie Sutton
Patrick "Panda" Leonard
Paul Willing
Kelly Zimmermann
The Johnson Family
Skye Norton

Ben shultz
Benjamin Grabham
Gerry Lee
Will Sanders
JZ
Kelley Ross
Kevin
Matthew Pemble
jethro wallace
Ryan Mucklin
Tristan Hams
Benjamin Leow
Bryan Pace
Rebecca Dominguez
Calin R Carter
Michelle Wang
Benoit
James Bryan
João Paulo Bonatelli
Sarah
Steven Rychetnik
Ahmed Mainul Bari
Landan S.
Nicole =^.^=
Big Bad Boston
Erin M
Nakia Sanchez
Gil Pettingell

Amanda Roberts

E. Tamar Alford	Tobster	Paul Arpaia
Sara M.	Jared	Ethan Glenn-Reller
Nick Jardine	Dan Pierson	Cole Whitney
Andreas M. Clauss	Jason Graffius	Kayak_chick
Trisha & Jeff Seaman	Eric Ortiz	Cesar de la Riva
Brendan Clougherty	Thomas Mögel	Carlos Díez-Gil
Karren R Orozco	David Rutledge	Kerry Kennedy
James Kaucher	Shaunda L Bowman	Tek Shen Ling
Holly Brown	Eric Tuennecke	Jolene Schleicher
Bernard De Santis III	Joschka Schaffner	Johnathan Rice
Erin Foster	Dave MacDonald	Nicole Lavallee
Anson Chan	Joshua Hislop	Matjaž Kraševec
Amber E	Eva Lo	Carlos Balthazar
Jacquelynn	Kate Ho	Daniel Kitayama
Denise Bos	L Zelnick	Chris L.
Ben & Rebecca Coffey	Roger Tjosås	David Donovan & Liu Nanxue
Ken Mencher	Sunny Thipsidakhom	Jil Shuen
Björn M	Falk A. Glade	Judith Stubenvoll
Richard Rossi	Maddie	Carrie
DP Viprakasit	Paul Lewis	Steven and Theresa Williams
Jessica Quezada	Yojan	Dom H.
Kevin J. Lee	David Nurbin	Danwool and Loob
Dr. Benitez	Mark H Webert	Diana Moritz
Gloria Fern	Jason Smulders	Andrea Noms Grefenstette
Thierry Corlieto	Zita Haglund	James Ruiz-Morales
Michael Brand	Dan & Emma	Crasy Dumplings I
Stephanie Ingram	Tom	Carolyn Brindle
D. Klemm	Nirven	David Miller

Crazy Dumplings

Luke Otlang	Rachel Droessler	Rebekah
Monkey King	Leah Zelnick	Stephenie Cheng-LaBoyne
Anon Y. Mous	Fionn Barker	Rhino horn is not medicine!
Mark e	Heather M. Hostetler	Vincent B. Donadio
Angelica Garrison	K Jacco	Targatt
Oliver J	Chris S.	Stefanie Hiu
Katherine S	Richard Fresow	Burgin Howdeshell
Snoozypanda	Alex Ambers	Richard F. Daley
Danielle Greene	Alison N.	Rachel Alystine
Annie Sylvain	Cristie Fagnano	Aleksandra Kuhl
John Gillespie	Tina & John Tipton	Charlotte C. Gauthier 42
Rod Perez [Mx]	Alison Benowitz	Lamb
Erin Rowett	Jupiter Talos	Laurie Kibbe
Angela Day	Bob	Jean Lee MC
Dajomu	Seow Wan Yi	Brandon Jablonski
Steve Impett	Alistair Morrison	John Clayton
Martyn Mendyuk	Alex Charles	R. Schäfer-Baehre
Hector Vega	Ineke Allez	J. C. Pombo
Alex Tsue	Samantha Douglass	Sara 'Bagel' Nagel
Richard Telford	Lisa E	H. Morgan
Nathan Kellen	Evan Morgan	Ann Foerster
Matt Tolle	Steve Eckart	Sophie V.T.
Max Peng	Mark Brown	Robert Farley
Mike	Jasmine	Greg "schmegs" Schwartz
Yayoi Natsume	Rosalie Reyes	Balazs Kosaras
Philip Jacobs	Kerry A. Vaughan	Alexander Y. Hawson
KJ Yuan	Nick Wang	Annette Widjaja
Clif Blanchard	Chris Atwood	Kevin Broger

Amanda Roberts

Jeremy Dorfschmidt	Jason L	Santiago Vites
Tim	Jonathan Meadowcroft	Chase Meyers
Dagur Bjarnason	Alexandra Arias	In the beggining
Amy Stewart	Kevin the murse	D Palmer
Whitney J Wadlow	Taeken	Glenn
S.E. Radcliff	Josephine Leong	Rich Gibson
Andrew McCarthy	Andrew Wiskin	Marcus "NeoAbsolution" Reed
Remko van Haften	Abby	Lady Cray Cray Dumplinger
Tracey	Catherine	Joe, Vanessa & Emmy Seliga
MelaGal	Sarah Kong	Chris and Kourtney Aikens
Andrea Lupien	Mike T	Elisabeth "Lizzie" Seaworth
Holly L	Toaster's mom	Welmoed the Home Inspector
Kathleen Tejeda	Ayrin Cooke	Stijn Hommes
sam	Ajen Limbu	Eadwin Tomlinson
Cheryl Wong	Tracy Dawicki	Sara Cornelison
¡Liz!	Julie Borthwick	Derek Sagima
Amanda Power	Andi	Savannah Chasing Hawk

Stephanie Wiener

Timo Glander & Ruowei Lei-Glander

I hope I understood the question correctly

Keith Stattenfield & Loretta Beavers

Brittany Greene & Jared Ruocco

Till min dotter Bianca Andretta Bacic

Fizzlewick Napoleon Orpheus Roarty Daedalus, Esq.

Caleb Koval (budding young chef)

Emily from www.emilyreadseverything.com

Daniel Gurfinkel and Irena Korotchenko

Delaney K. Anderson, MSW